Praise for *The P*

"*The Persistent God* is a beautiful text full of engaging stories, a breadth of different methods, and practical insights on developing your own best approach. It starts out light and easy but continues to go deeper and richer with every new chapter. You'll want to keep rereading it with each new stage of your own spiritual growth."
—**Joshua Danis**, head of parish and diocesan partnerships, Hallow, and author of *Living the Fruit of the Spirit: How God's Grace Can Transform Your World*

"In *The Persistent God*, there is something for everyone. This includes young teenagers beginning to pray or octogenarians. We learn of Fr. Albert's early encounter with our persistent God at fourteen years of age. He also beautifully weaves the stories of others seeking God. It is a book to be read from cover-to-cover but then referred to when one enters dryness, darkness, or the other challenges of life. This book should have a privileged place on the bookshelf of anyone serious about the journey of prayer!"
—**Sr. Mary Connor, OSC**, president of Holy Name Federation of Poor Clare Monasteries

"What a gift! Fr. Albert Haase has offered us a wonderful approach to prayer that is accessible to anyone, anywhere. God is knocking on the door of your heart—welcome him in and prepare to see your spiritual life grow and deepen. This beautiful, practical and inspiring book will be a blessing for so many. I know I'll be returning to it often!"
—**Deacon Greg Kandra**, author of *The Busy Person's Guide to Prayer*

"Thorough and accessible, even those skilled in prayer will refresh their sensitivity to the Lord's voice through *The Persistent God*. Fr. Haase, with simplicity and wisdom, offers practical direction on technique and method, seasons of prayer such as aridity and desolation, along with questions for reflection to aid readers in their quest for a deeper prayer life. The abundance of personal stories from his decades of experience are especially helpful in putting a face to the soul seeking the face of God in prayer."
—**Elizabeth Kelly**, author of *A Place Called Golgotha*, retreat director, LizK.org.

"With kindness, gentle guidance, and simplicity, Fr. Haase has provided an invaluable handbook to animate our prayer life. In *The Persistent God: A Guide to Deepening Prayer*, Fr. Haase not only offers a practical introduction to many different approaches to prayer, but also shares his wise and sensitive counsel on the typical obstacles we encounter in our journey with God. Like St. Thérèse of Lisieux, he encourages us to pray the way we can, not the way we can't. This is one book I will keep close at hand!"
—**Marisa Guerin, PhD**, coauthor of *Life Lessons from St. Thérèse of Lisieux*

"Fr. Haase's book is comprehensive without being overwhelming, deep yet always accessible, and richly peppered with vignettes from the lives of his spiritual directees. Both beginners in the life of prayer and long-term pilgrims on the way will find his writing insightful, motivational, and indispensable."
—**Rabbi Stuart Dauermann, PhD**, director of Interfaithfulness and author of *Eat This Book: Strength for Your Journey With the Jewish Jesus*

ALBERT HAASE, OFM

THE PERSISTENT

GOD

A GUIDE TO
DEEPENING PRAYER

theWORD
among us®
press

Published by The Word Among Us Press
7115 Guilford Drive, Suite 100, Frederick, Maryland 21704

wau.org

28 27 26 25 24   1 2 3 4 5

ISBN: 978-1-59325-720-0

eISBN: 978-1-59325-721-7

Design by Rose Audette

Library of Congress Control Number: 2023924038

"In that city there was a widow who kept coming to [the judge] and saying, 'Grant me justice against my opponent.'" (Luke 18:3)

"Listen! I am standing at the door, knocking; if you hear my voice and open the door, I will come in to you." (Revelation 3:20)

Contents

Introduction

A few months after my fourteenth birthday, I became aware of a desire: I wanted a relationship with God that went beyond mere Sunday Mass attendance. Now, more than five decades later, that desire, which I subsequently discovered was placed in my heart by God, has confirmed me in my baptismal call to mission.

When I first became aware of that desire as a teenager, I sought Fr. Murray's advice.

"How do I start a relationship with God?" I asked.

"The spiritual tradition mentions three specific practices," he said. "They are prayer, fasting, and almsgiving." As soon as he said that, I remembered that Jesus had mentioned them explicitly as well (see Matthew 6:1-18).

I didn't have much luck with fasting. On the days when I attempted it, I found myself thinking more about the tacos of earth than the treasures of heaven. I hesitated with almsgiving because I didn't have much money. I had yet to learn that almsgiving is not just about sharing your treasure; it includes your time and talents as well.

When I told him about my false starts, Fr. Murray encouraged me. "Why don't you try prayer?" he asked. "Make the commitment to spend some time with God every day. You could start with a Rosary. Once you finish it, you could pray for your family and friends. Or maybe you could start with spiritual reading. Pick out a book and read each paragraph slowly. Once you come to the end of the paragraph, pause and reflect on what you read. And then continue with the next paragraph."

I was intrigued and attracted to the idea of spiritual reading. It appeared easy and doable. And so, at age fourteen, I made the commitment to embark on the spiritual journey with daily spiritual reading. I decided to do it for an hour. I've been faithful to that decision for more than half a century. The only thing that has changed and evolved over the years is how I spend that hour.

Like the Persistent Widow

Over the years, my hour of prayer has revealed to me two important biblical truths about God. Both are rooted in the New Testament: one from a parable by Jesus found in the Gospel of Luke; the other from words spoken by the risen Christ to the church of Laodicea found in the Book of Revelation.

The beginning of the eighteenth chapter of Luke's Gospel explores one of Jesus' teachings about prayer. Found only in the third Gospel and called either the Unjust Judge or the Persistent Widow, this Lucan parable is introduced with the Evangelist's interpretation of it. He writes, "Then Jesus told them a parable about their need to pray always and not to lose heart" (18:1). Having set up the reader for his interpretation, Luke offers the parable:

> In a certain city there was a judge who neither feared God nor had respect for people. In that city there was a widow who kept coming to him and saying, "Grant me justice against my opponent." For a while he refused, but later he said to himself, "Though I have no fear of God and no respect for anyone, yet because this widow keeps bothering me, I will grant her justice, so that she may not wear me out by continually coming." (Luke 18:2-5)

In a bold move rarely seen in the four Gospels, Luke has Jesus interpret his own parable. He buttresses the interpretation by referring to Jesus as "the Lord" (18:6), thus highlighting the importance and accuracy of the interpretation. Not surprisingly, the divine interpretation matches the Evangelist's (see 18:1). Using a rhetorical technique of deduction, where something that applies in a lesser case must also apply in a more important one, the Lord makes clear that if an unjust judge who cares nothing for God or others will grant the plea of a widow who persists in her request, how much more will God, who is thoroughly just and loving, grant justice to someone asking for it.

Though I am not a trained Scripture scholar, I understand that the attraction to Jesus' parables lies in their multifaceted interpretations. Like short stories or poems, parables can mean different things to different people. There's no one "correct" way to explain or interpret them. That's their power and perennial appeal.

For many years, Luke's interpretation, carefully nuanced by the Lord, left me a bit baffled and confused. How could God be the judge since, in his own words, he had "no fear of God and no respect for anyone" (18:4)? It's odd that God would have no self-respect or esteem for others. Furthermore, associating God with the judge makes God seem like a petty deity who needs to be cajoled and strong-armed. Finally, and more important, God, if he's the parable's judge, responds to our nagging petitions for justice just to get us off his back. This certainly is not the loving Father revealed to us by Jesus.

Is there another possible interpretation that could remain faithful to the explanation that the purpose of this parable is to promote continual prayer and fervor? Some contemporary Catholic Scripture scholars offer us one: God is like the persistent widow, and we are like the unjust judge. As we grow in fidelity to daily prayer, we discover how every day, God comes into our lives and asks, prompts, and even persistently cajoles us to respond to a particular need that helps promote the kingdom of peace, love, and justice. Daily prayer strengthens our baptismal call to mission.

The Knock on the Door of the Heart

The second biblical truth about God that I've discovered in prayer comes from the Book of Revelation. In the third chapter, the risen Christ speaks to the church in Laodicea. Though rich in material wealth, the Laodiceans were lukewarm in their baptismal obligation to witness to their Christian faith. They feared rejection, suffering, and even possible death. In this context, the risen Christ says to them, "Listen! I am standing at the door, knocking; if you hear my voice and open the door, I will come in to you" (Revelation 3:20). The risen Christ is calling them to risk opening the door of their hearts and become vulnerable for his sake. Daily prayer heightens our awareness of the persistent divine knock and the call to open the door of our hearts to God.

The Persistent God: A Guide to Deepening Prayer explores the unrelenting divine invitation to a deeper relationship that goes beyond mere Sunday Mass attendance. In responding to that invitation, we not only learn to become vulnerable with God but also discover deeper dimensions of our baptismal calling.

You'll meet some interesting people in these pages whom I have been privileged to sit with in spiritual direction. To ensure my spiritual directees' privacy, I've changed their names and the details of their stories.

It's my hope that this little book will entice and encourage you to open the door of your heart to a God who, like the persistent widow in Jesus' parable, calls each one of us to help build the kingdom of peace, love, and justice.

Albert Haase, OFM
Feast of the Sacred Heart of Jesus

1

GROWING IN PRAYERFULNESS

Prayer should make me prayerful.

As a fourteen-year-old, I enthusiastically embraced a reflective method of spiritual reading: Read a few sentences. Pause. Reflect. Read. Sometimes the hour would fly by. Sometimes it would chug along. And sometimes I spent more time looking at the clock than reflecting on what I had just read. But I was faithful to the daily practice, and occasionally checking in with my spiritual director, Fr. Murray, proved helpful and encouraging. I took undue delight—maybe even pride—in "getting my prayer time in." It was a task that I could check off my daily to-do list.

Then in my late twenties, after my prayer time had morphed and evolved from spiritual reading to a mixture of the slow recitation of the Jesus Prayer ("Lord, Jesus Christ, Son of the Living God, have mercy on me, a sinner") combined with prayers of intercession and petition, I was stopped in my tracks. Sr. Teresa, my spiritual director at the time, gently prodded me, "Albert, daily prayer is not simply a task to be completed but also a continuing attitude to be fostered. What happens after the hour of prayer is more important than the hour itself."

I instantly recognized Sr. Teresa's wisdom, but it would take another twenty years to discover its practical implications.

"

Prayer should make us prayerful—that is, aware and mindful of the daily presence and divine invitations of God.

From Prayer to Prayerfulness

We need to be faithful to prayer and spiritual practices because they help to make us sensitive to how God comes and knocks on the heart's door in the ordinary moments of our nitty-gritty lives. In other words, prayer should make us prayerful—that is, aware and mindful of the daily presence and divine invitations of God. As Sr. Teresa wisely noted, "What happens *after* the hour of prayer is more important than the hour itself."

And what happens after our prayer time is action. If our prayerfulness does not affect how we live and help build God's kingdom of peace, love, and justice, then we have constructed a shallow, superficial, and sham spirituality. Jesus compares this kind of paralyzed prayerfulness to a foolish man who builds his house on sand (see Matthew 7:26-27). The Letter of James likens it to a man who looks at himself in the mirror, goes away, and promptly forgets what he looks like (see James 1:23-24). Prayer, prayerfulness, and action form an undivided trinity.

In this regard, Jesus tells a compelling parable commonly called the Judgment of the Nations that suggests two important points (see Matthew 25:31-46). First, the sheep—also referred to as "the righteous" (25:37)—inherit the kingdom because their prayer blossomed into a prayerfulness that gave birth to acts of charity toward the hungry, the thirsty, the stranger, the naked, the sick, and those in prison. Righteousness is when the act of prayer, the attitude of prayerfulness, and the action of charity form a coherent whole. The goats, on the other hand, are sent into eternal punishment because, in the words of the Son of Man, "I was hungry and you gave me no food, I was thirsty and you gave me nothing to drink, I was a stranger and you did not welcome me, naked and you did not give me clothing, sick and in prison and you did not visit me" (25:42-43). The latter are an example of shallow spirituality and paralyzed prayerfulness.

Second, the Son of Man—later referred to as "the king" (Matthew 25:34, 40)—directly identifies himself as the hungry, thirsty, stranger, naked, sick, and prisoner. The sheep's questions, "Lord, when was it that we saw you hungry and gave you food, or thirsty and gave you something to drink? And when was it that we saw you a stranger and welcomed you, or naked and gave you clothing? And when was it that we saw you sick or in prison and visited you?" (25:37-39), clearly indicate they simply were responding to the immediate need before them, not knowing the person to whom they were ministering was the kingdom's sovereign. The point is obvious: God is a God of surprise and disguise who, like the persistent widow in Jesus' parable (see Luke 18:1-5), is constantly calling us to build the kingdom with acts of peace, love, and justice in the nitty-gritty of our daily lives.

The Megaphone of Our Lives

How does this God of surprise and disguise make his presence known? How does God invite our response for the sake of the kingdom? Through the megaphone called our lives. That megaphone consists of the four dimensions of human experience. Though we need to be attentive to all four dimensions, everyone learns over time that God has a preferred dimension for each individual.

James is one of those people who lives with his feet planted firmly on the ground. He has learned that God likes to speak to him through the physical dimension of life: his body's gut reaction to situations, his deepest feelings, creation, and the situations in which he finds himself. I remember him telling me that he once watched a turtle go into its shell. "At that very instant, my gut told me that I needed to take the time to reflect and meditate on what was going on in my life. I do that every day now. I call it my 'shell time.'"

God uses a different preferred dimension with Stephanie. She hears God knocking on the door of her heart primarily in the social dimension of life. "Over the years, I've learned that when family members or friends independently tell me the same thing or give me the same advice, that's God's way of getting my attention. I listen to what they are saying even when it stings."

Many people are attentive to the spiritual dimension of life as God's preferred dimension to communicate with them. At fourteen years of age, I became sensitive to God through spiritual reading. Over time, that expanded to public prayer and liturgy, sermons and homilies, and private prayer and personal devotions.

Edward is very sensitive to the mental dimension of life. For him, this includes his hunches and intuitions, his imagination, his reason, and even reflecting on his past. He keeps a notebook beside his bed in which he records his dreams. "It never ceases to amaze me how God teaches me about myself through dreams," he says as he opens his dream notebook and shares with me a dream of particular significance.

Over the years, I have come to appreciate Sr. Teresa's statement that prayer is an attitude to be fostered. Like many people, when I first responded to God's knocking on the door of my heart and his request to be intentional about daily prayer, I thought of my prayer time as sticking my ears up in the clouds so I could hear the voice of God. But I ever-so-gradually discovered that if I really wanted to experience God's presence, invitations, and requests in my life, I needed to keep my ears to the ground and, like the righteous sheep, respond to the immediate need before me. I must listen to my life and its four dimensions. Like Mary, the mother of Jesus, I have to treasure and ponder all my experiences in the heart (see Luke 2:51).

Pastor Joe's Ten-Minute Prayer

As you read this book, you'll discover numerous ways to treasure and ponder your experiences. Hopefully, your reflections will help you open the door of your heart, grow in the prayerful awareness of the divine, and respond to God's invitation to help build the kingdom. Let's explore three practical prayer techniques that help to foster that prayerful and responsive attitude toward life.

Joe is the pastor of a large Baptist church. A few years ago, his clergy support group decided to read and reflect on the Carmelite Brother Lawrence of the Resurrection's *The Practice of the Presence of God*. Joe was intrigued by the idea of intentionally calling to mind the presence of God and doing everything in the divine presence. He tried it but quickly became frustrated. "I kept getting distracted and losing my awareness of God," he told me.

He soon found a way that has proven helpful for him. Six times a day—when he wakes up, at 9 a.m., 12 noon, 3 p.m., 6 p.m., and before retiring—he deliberately sits in a chair, closes his eyes, takes a few deep breaths, and then for ten minutes calls to mind God's presence.

"I remind myself that God is like the air I breathe. I don't see the air, but it surrounds me. So, too, in God I live and move and have my being," he told me as he quoted Paul's line from the sermon in the Areopagus (see Acts 17:28). He added, "I think of my ten-minute prayer as a way to recharge my spiritual battery. And I've noticed that by doing it six times a day, God has become the background music in my life. This works better for me than one prolonged prayer period of sixty minutes."

When Pastor Joe used the air and background music metaphors for God, it suddenly dawned on me that he had discovered the secret to understanding Paul's curious admonition to "pray without ceasing" (1 Thessalonians 5:17). Paul is not challenging us to constantly mutter prayers. That would be humanly impossible. Rather, he is challenging us to live with an ongoing spirit of contemplative devotion, with prayerfulness, with treasuring and listening to the events of our lives. When prayer give birth to prayerfulness, we begin to think of God being as close to us as air or as the background music of daily life—and coming to us in the surprising disguise of the hungry, thirsty, stranger, naked, sick, and prisoner.

Is your prayer making you prayerful? Does the fruit of your prayer time spill out into your time with the person next to you on the commuter train or in the board meeting or while you are loading the dishwasher, waiting on customers, or driving the kids to soccer practice? If so, I suggest you have discovered Pastor Joe's answer to St. Paul's admonition. If not, you might want to try another prayer technique.

The Examen

There's a second technique that fosters a reflective awareness of God's presence in daily life. It relies on a five-hundred-year-old tradition. It was first proposed by the founder of the Society of Jesus (the Jesuits), Ignatius of Loyola. It's called the Examen.

Three preliminary comments are worthy of note. Ignatius suggested that the Examen be done twice a day, once before lunch and once before retiring. But, being a master of flexibility, he noted that if a person cannot do it twice a day, once is sufficient. To experience its fruitfulness, it should be practiced daily. "There's no vacation from the Examen," I was advised.

Second, this prayer is prayed by the clock—fifteen to twenty minutes at most. It is not necessary to get through all five steps in every prayer period. An Ignatian scholar wisely told me, "The genius of this teaching is that Ignatius wants us to stay where the grace of God keeps us. So if today, for example, God's grace wants you to linger on step 1 for the entire prayer time, then stay there. Don't think that you must get through all five steps in a single prayer period. But you always start with step 1 even if yesterday you only got to step 2 or 3."

Third, a person should never feel compelled to stick to the order of the five steps as Ignatius proposed them. Once individuals have practiced the Examen for a while, they are free to change the order of the steps to their own liking. "Make it your own," a Jesuit priest told me.

The Examen consists of five steps:

- It begins with *gratitude*. Since the last time I have practiced the Examen, for what am I grateful? Maybe I received a surprise phone call, a text, or an email from someone I haven't heard from in a long time. Maybe I was given a gift. Perhaps I was touched by the beauty of the sunrise or the wonder of a child. Maybe I found some hope and consolation to face a challenging situation. I look over the previous hours for the blessings of the day and thank God.

- If I haven't used up all the time allotted, I move to the *prayer to the Holy Spirit*. "I say a simple prayer," a young Jesuit told me. "I ask the Holy Spirit to heal me of my blindness, deafness, and hard-heartedness so that as I review the hours since I last prayed the Examen, I might see, hear, and experience the presence of God in my day." This second step acknowledges the importance and centrality of the Holy Spirit in the life of the Christian. Think of the Holy Spirit as the operating system of our spiritual lives.

- If there is still time available, I will continue with the review. This is the heart and soul of the Examen. I rummage through the details of the preceding hours and search for the presence of God. Keeping my ears to the ground, I listen for those moments when God was challenging, prodding, or urging me to respond to a particular situation that would have helped manifest the kingdom characteristics of peace, love, and justice. I ask myself how God was present and active in my daily routine today.

- Ignatius's fourth step of the Examen is the *dialogue of forgiveness*. I express my sorrow for being blind, deaf, and hard-hearted to God's presence and requests. Because it's a dialogue, after expressing my sorrow and regret, I wait to hear God's response. And the divine response is always one of forgiveness, understanding, and compassion. God gets the final word in the dialogue. As one Ignatian scholar told me, "If you leave the fourth step feeling guilty, you haven't done it correctly. Our forgiving God gets the final word."

- The Examen concludes, when time permits, with the *renewal*. This final step is about renewing and reaffirming my intention to be prayerful, to being attentive to God's presence and invitations in the ordinary moments of my daily life. I look over tomorrow's calendar. As best as I can predict, I ask myself where God might catch me unawares with a visit. In this final step, I remind myself that, as the sheep and goats discovered in the parable of the Judgment of the Nations, God is a God of surprise and disguise and never makes an appointment! I need to keep an eye out for God.

The Daily Check-In

Eric designed a spin-off to the Examen that he calls "the daily check-in."

"After I wake up and am brushing my teeth and taking a shower, I deliberately remind myself that God is going to visit me today. I can't sleepwalk through my day. I need to be intentional about staying awake and recognizing how God visits me. This is a way to reboot my spiritual awareness and mindfulness. I think of it as drinking a cup of spiritual caffeine.

"Then right before lunch, I quickly review the past few hours. *Where was God? How did God manifest his presence to me? Was I aware of him when he presented himself to me?* I spend three or four minutes looking over the morning.

"In the evening, I ask the same questions about my afternoon. I then conclude with a prayer of adoration and thanksgiving for God's abiding presence in my life."

Prayer should never devolve into a simple task that should be done and checked off a daily to-do list. Rather, it should foster a prayerful awareness and contemplative mindfulness of the myriad ways God comes into our lives. That's the secret to understanding Paul's advice to pray unceasingly (see 1 Thessalonians 5:17). That can happen by following Pastor Joe's periodic prayer stops during the day, practicing the Examen, or using Eric's daily check-in. No matter what method we use, the goal is to listen for God's knock, open the door of the heart, and respond to the divine invitation or request.

REFLECTION QUESTIONS

1. How has my approach to prayer helped or hindered growth in a prayerful stance toward everyday activities?

2. Of the four dimensions of human experience, which is the one God prefers to use as the primary means of communication with me? When did God surprise me by using a different dimension?

3. Which of the prayer methods mentioned in this chapter might be advantageous and helpful for me?

2

FINDING MY METHOD

I need to find my own way to pray.

F rank holds a master's degree in art. I was amazed by his answer to my question about the wide array of painting styles. "Over the years, many different ones have emerged. A group of artists in Paris in the nineteenth century gave birth to Impressionism. They painted ordinary subject matter using relatively small, thin, yet visible brush strokes that emphasized an accurate depiction of light in its changing qualities. They often painted from an unusual visual angle and included movement as a crucial element of human perception and experience. Think of the paintings of Claude Monet or Vincent van Gogh's *The Starry Night*.

"Artists like Georges Seurat and Paul Signac branched off from Impressionism and started a technique, originally criticized, called Pointillism. Their technique, focused on a specific style of brushwork to apply the paint, relies on the ability of the viewer's eyes and mind to blend the color spots into a fuller range of tones. Have you seen a picture of Georges Seurat's *A Sunday on La Grande Jatte—1884* that depicts people from different social classes strolling and relaxing in a park just west of Paris? It's the classic example.

"The early twentieth century gave birth to the avant-garde movement called Cubism. Pablo Picasso and Georges Braque, for example, analyzed their subjects, broke them up, and then reassembled them in an abstract

"

EACH ONE OF US MUST FIND A PRAYER METHOD OR TECHNIQUE THAT HELPS US BE ATTENTIVE TO GOD'S PRESENCE, KNOCK, AND REQUESTS.

"

form, portraying the subject from multiple perspectives to give the subject a greater context.

"After World War I, Salvador Dalí and others developed Surrealism that depicted unnerving, illogical scenes and developed techniques to allow the unconscious mind to express itself."

As Frank continued, describing Abstract Expressionism and Abstract Art, my mind began to wander as I reflected on how artists respond in different ways to the subject of their paintings.

An Apt Metaphor

The different schools of painting provide a metaphor for how each one of us prays. The way we pray is our way of picking up the brush, rubbing it in the palette we have chosen, and approaching the canvas.

The challenge for anyone wanting to begin and nurture a relationship with God is to find a suitable and satisfying way to stand at the heart's door and open it when God, like the persistent widow in Jesus's parable (see Luke 18:1-5), knocks. Just as artists are creatively challenged to find a school of painting that expresses their heart and soul, so each one of us must find a prayer method or technique that helps us be attentive to God's presence, knock, and requests. Unfortunately, spiritual directors can easily take too much for granted. I learned that lesson yet again a few years ago.

"How do I begin to pray?" Cheri asked me as we began a spiritual direction relationship that would last for three years. Her question immediately reminded me of a request made two thousand years earlier when one of the disciples saw Jesus conclude his prayer, approached him, and said, "Lord, teach us to pray, as John taught his disciples" (Luke 11:1). My response to Cheri's question was ill-advised.

"Start with a simple prayer word. Maybe use 'love' or 'peace' or 'holy presence.' Say it very slowly as you breathe in and out. And then pause. Ponder the presence of God that surrounds you like the air you breathe. And when you get distracted—it'll happen very quickly—go back and slowly repeat the prayer word three or four times. Then pause again. Ponder the presence of God. And when you get distracted—I guarantee you, it will still happen again—go back and deliberately repeat the prayer word a few times. Then pause again until you are distracted. Do this for fifteen or twenty minutes every day. We can discuss the results at our next spiritual direction session." I felt confident that Cheri would enjoy this prayer technique.

The following month, Cheri was quick to tell me about her experience. "It didn't feel like prayer to me. It was more like a relaxation technique. It didn't give me the opportunity to talk to God and tell him what's on my mind or in my heart. Was I doing something wrong?"

Cheri's experience with my method of prayer reminded me again that everyone prays in a different way. When we forget that and think we do pray in the same way, it's like asking Picasso to paint like Monet or vice versa. Just as artists respond to their subject in a different way, so too we respond to God in our own unique way. Nurturing a relationship with God is a highly personal and intimate affair. What works for me obviously did not work for Cheri. And what may have worked for Cheri may not work for me.

When we become intentional about nurturing a relationship with God, our first task is to find our own way to pray. We discover that method by trial and error. Once we find our technique, we practice it and never apologize for it.

Methods and Techniques Abound

I'll be explaining some of the time-honored ways to pray throughout this book. As I discuss them, be aware that the best way to pray is the way that works for you. Sometimes that means strictly following the method. Other times, it might mean tweaking it in a way that is more conducive for you to respond to God's knocking on the door of your heart.

The most common method is *communal prayer*. Deacon Mark and his wife enjoy praying the Liturgy of the Hours together every morning and evening. Consisting of psalms, a short Scripture reading, and intercessions, this prayer technique helps them not only to solidify their life as a couple but also to feel a part of the universal Church, as clergy and religious pray it also, sometimes individually and sometimes in community.

Louise has found the group recitation of the Rosary meaningful. "I was never a Rosary person," she confessed to me, "until the pandemic of 2020. I was looking for a community to connect with while we were all in lockdown. I had nowhere to turn. And then a friend told me about a group of people across the country who gather three times a week via Zoom to pray the Rosary. I joined the group, and now with people from California to Connecticut, we pray and intercede for our and the world's intentions."

Many people enjoy the celebration of the sacraments, especially the Eucharist and Reconciliation, to grow in attentiveness to God. Opening the door of the heart to the words of Scripture proclaimed in the Mass readings can be either invigorating or unsettling. Experiencing Christ in the Real Presence and in his ministry of forgiveness can spur one to opening wider the door of the heart.

I believe communal prayer in some way, shape, or form should be part and parcel of every person's spiritual life. Why? Because communal prayer is a reminder that we never walk the spiritual journey alone. Nor is the journey just about "me and God." Christianity is a family affair, and a spiritual life without community is a caricature.

Praying with Scripture

But I am also a strong proponent of spending time in *private prayer*. This also helps to hone our skills in awareness and sensitivity to the myriad ways God, like the persistent widow in Jesus's parable (see Luke 18:1-5), knocks on the door of the heart (see Revelation 3:20). Let's look at some of these private methods of prayer that promote prayerfulness.

Early in the history of Christian spirituality—it's impossible to discover when it first started—believers turned to the Scriptures for inspiration. By the late third and early fourth centuries, desert dwellers were slowly—sometimes silently, sometimes in a low voice—repeating the words of Scripture as they wove reed mats to sell and support themselves. "Be pleased, O God, to deliver me. O LORD, make haste to help me!" (Psalm 70:1) was a favorite verse. "Be still, and know that I am God! I am exalted among the nations, I am exalted in the earth" (Psalm 46:10) was another one. Marsha was delighted to discover this, and now, as she folds clothes, dices vegetables, and vacuums the carpet, she joins the practice of these ancient Christians of the Egyptian and Palestinian deserts.

Another simple scriptural prayer, suitable for slow recitation and meditation, was written down around the seventh century. Called the Jesus Prayer, its versions include "Jesus, Son of God, have mercy on me," "Jesus, have mercy on me, a sinner," "Jesus, mercy," and "*Kyrie eleison*" ("Lord, have mercy"). This prayer is premised on the biblical beliefs that God's name is conceived as the place of his presence, and knowledge of the name is evidence of a relationship with God (see Exodus 3:13-15). The prayer's roots can be found in what scholars believe to be a line from an early baptismal hymn found in the second chapter of the Letter to the Philippians ("Jesus Christ is Lord," verse 11), Gabriel's explanation of how Mary was to conceive in Luke's Gospel ("Son of God," 1:35), the prayer of the tax collector in the parable of the Pharisee and the Tax Collector, "God, be merciful to me, a sinner!" (Luke 18:13), and the cry of a blind beggar recorded in Luke 18:38 ("Jesus, Son of David, have mercy on me!"). I'll have more to say about the practice of this prayer in chapter 6.

The mid-eleventh century gave birth to a prominent prayer still popular and often identified as exclusively Catholic. It begins with two verses from Scripture, both spoken to the Virgin Mary: it repeats Gabriel's words to her at the Annunciation, "Hail Mary, full of grace, the Lord is with thee" (see Luke 1:28), and Elizabeth's subsequent words to her, "Blessed art thou among women and blessed is the fruit of thy womb" (see Luke 1:42). By the late-fifteenth and mid-sixteenth centuries, a petition was added that invoked the continued help and assistance of the Virgin now and at the hour of death. Although pious tradition attributes the rosary on which the Hail Mary is prayed as a gift of the Blessed Mother to Dominic of Osma in 1215, the recitation of fifty to one hundred and fifty Hail Marys seems to have existed two centuries earlier. Though unaware of its rich history, Trappist monk Br. Juan prays it daily "as a way to honor the first disciple of Jesus and to be led into the presence of her Son."

The slow and deliberate recitation of a favorite scriptural verse can be a wonderful asset to promoting and maintaining a spirit of prayerfulness and devotion. It can sharpen our hospitality when God appears at the door of the heart.

Lectio Divina

There are two other techniques that have proven helpful for praying with Scripture.

The twelfth-century monastic tradition gave birth to a form of scriptural prayer commonly referred to by its Latin name *lectio divina* ("sacred reading"). Traditionally, this technique consists of four steps.

- First, I *read* a short biblical text three or four times to get the gist of what it is saying. I want to consider any footnotes associated with the passage to help clarify and understand its meaning.

- Next, I *meditate* on the passage. The monastic tradition used the image of "chewing" the words like a cow chewing its cud. Using another image, I treat the words of the passage as serum in an intravenous drip that I allow in my veins to reenergize me. Still another image considers Scripture as the wind in an open-windowed room that rearranges the papers on my desk. Part of my rumination on the passage includes what the passage says to me, how it strikes me emotionally, and what words or phrases, if any, jump off the page for me.

- After a few minutes, I move to the third step, which is to *pray*. As a response to my meditation in step 2, this prayer can be one of thanksgiving, praise, wonder, or even confession of my guilt. It might even consist of the slow recitation of a word or phrase that gave me cause to pause.

- The fourth and final step is to *contemplate*. I pause in silence and let the passage, my reflection on it, and my prayer wash over me.

- Some of my spiritual directees like to add a fifth step and that is to *act* upon the passage. I strategize for a concrete way to put flesh and bones on what this passage has encouraged me to complete, continue, or change in my thoughts, words, or deeds.

I must confess that I have struggled with this traditional method of sacred reading. I can do the first three steps, but the fourth step always leaves me dissatisfied and mystified. I get distracted with thoughts about what exactly I am supposed to be doing and if I am contemplating correctly. Consequently, like an artist branching off from one school of painting to start another, I've branched off to start another "school" of *lectio divina*. You can remember it as the "Four Hs."

My approach starts off in the traditional way. I read the passage a few times as well as the footnotes. Once I have grasped the flow of the plot, if it's a story from the Gospels or the message of the letter's passage, I ask myself four questions.

- *What does this passage say to my history?* I reflect on how this story or passage might correspond to or intersect with an event or incident in my life, either past or present. Maybe there was a time when I, like the hemorrhaging woman, was desperate for a healing; when I, like the rich young man, wanted a deeper spiritual life; when I, like the woman caught in adultery, had my sin made public. Maybe I struggled with the tension between obedience to the law and a response of love and compassion, or read a poem or heard a song about the characteristics of love.

- *What does this passage say to my head?* I mine the story or passage for information and insights into God's relationship with me and ponder their meaning and implication. This knowledge sometimes confirms, expands, or challenges my current understanding of the faith and the spiritual journey.

- Third, *what does this passage say to my heart?* I monitor my emotional reaction and my feelings toward the information and insights I have received from the first two questions. Questions 2 and 3 will sometimes lead me to a conversation with God.

- Finally, *what does this passage say to my hands?* I reflect on how I will live the message of this passage in my daily life. My proposed action might come from God's desire or encouragement. Without an answer to this fourth question, my engagement with the sacred text is shallow and superficial. As Jesus reminded his disciples, "My mother and my brothers are those who hear the word of God and *do* it" (Luke 8:21, emphasis mine). As I mentioned in the previous chapter, prayer, prayerfulness, and action form an undivided trinity.

Praying the Four Hs—history, head, heart, hands—is another way to practice *lectio divina* and discover God's invitation to help build the kingdom of peace, love, and justice.

Imaginative Prayer

Besides *lectio divina*, there is a second technique to engage the word of God, particularly scenes from the four Gospels. Five hundred years ago, Ignatius of Loyola presented it as a means for spiritual transformation. It unabashedly uses the imagination and one's creativity to engage a Gospel story.

As with *lectio divina*, I read the Gospel story a few times to know the plot of the story and understand its flow.

- I then pause to consider the characters in the story. Who are they? What motivations and emotions might they have brought to this scene?

- I continue by entering the scene and visualizing it. How's the weather—rainy, cloudy, or clear? How are people dressed? What are their moods like—calm and collected or anxious or desperate or judgmental? What emotions and feelings are elicited by Jesus and the people involved in the scene, including the onlookers? I use my imagination and creativity to capture this scene and place myself in it.

- The heart of imaginative prayer is assuming the role of one of the characters in the story's plot. Perhaps I assume the role of Jesus or the paralytic or busy Martha or the grieving woman of Nain or one of the onlookers. How do I respond to this scene? What emotions or thoughts arise? Does this scene remind me of something from my past? Or maybe the plot changes from the Gospel's rendition as I ponder, play, and pray it in my imagination. Why do I think it has changed? I take my time with this step.

- Some people find it helpful to journal after composing the scene and acting in it. The noted thoughts, feelings, and memories might be helpful material to bring and process with a spiritual director.
- I conclude my imaginative prayer with a prayer to God that summarizes my insights, thoughts, and feelings.

"But how can this be prayer? It's all based upon my fantasy," Peter noted. I responded by telling him how modern science reminds us of the influence of our minds on our lives. What we think about matters in our spiritual development. Our thoughts can profoundly affect our emotions, passions, and actions. God is not averse to using our intellectual, emotional, or sensual faculties to invite us to open the door of the heart a bit wider.

I don't have an active imagination, so the traditional practice of imaginative prayer doesn't suit me. But I have found it helpful to engage the story by treating it as a metaphor for a situation from my past or present. As I meditate on Jesus walking on water toward the disciples in a boat caught in a storm, I recall moments when I felt like I was in a storm at sea and experienced the presence of God in the midst of my emotional storm. Reflecting on Jesus being betrayed by Judas' kiss, I ponder those times when I have been betrayed by a friend or relative. The raising of Lazarus invites me to recall times when a relationship I thought was over suddenly came back to life or a moment when I felt reenergized after a failure, thanks to Jesus' relationship to me. The story of Martha and Mary reminds me of times when, even though I love my siblings, friction came between us. I've been amazed at some insights that have arisen when I treat the Gospel story as a metaphor or analogy for my own experience.

ACTS

"Some of the prayer techniques you've mentioned seem a bit impersonal and mechanical to me. I want something more personal and individualized, something that will let me talk with God and tell him what's going on in my life."

I responded to Amy's objection by teaching her a form of personalized prayer easily remembered by the acronym ACTS. It has four distinct movements.

- This prayer begins with *adoration*. I acknowledge the Blessed Trinity as the center of my life. I worship God and say a prayer that glorifies the Father, Son, and Holy Spirit. Some people like to slowly repeat the "Holy, Holy, Holy" from Mass a couple of times. The prayer of adoration is a practical way to call to mind the presence of God that surrounds me like the air I breathe.

- The second movement is *confession*. I look over the preceding hours in light of my Christian discipleship. When did I allow my worry and anxiety to sabotage my peace and joy? When could I have been kinder and more charitable, generous, and loving? When did I give in to my desires and passions in an inappropriate way? When did my ego rear its head and seek unrealistic demands? When did I allow a hurt or grudge to influence my reaction to someone? When could I have been more forgiving and compassionate? How could I have made God's kingdom of peace, love, and justice more visible? Having made an examination of conscience, I confess my sins and failures to God. I conclude with the Act of Contrition. This movement also reminds me that, sinner though I am, I am still a beloved child of God.

- That knowledge of being God's beloved child leads me to spend time in *thanksgiving*. I acknowledge everything as a gift from God. Sometimes this thanksgiving will be focused on the major events of my life, for example, meeting my spouse, the birth of a child, finding a satisfying occupation, or receiving successful medical care. Other times, this movement might be focused on an event that happened in the preceding hours: a text from a friend, a word of encouragement, or a satisfying interview. This third movement is an explicit reminder that in the presence of God, I can claim nothing as my own—except for my sin. Everything else is grace, gift, and blessing.

- I conclude this prayer period with *supplication*. I petition God for my personal intentions: doing well on an upcoming exam, having a better relationship with a family member or friend, or finding the courage to make a difficult decision. I also intercede to God for family members and friends for whom I have promised to pray: "That Jill's health improves"; "That Billy can find a suitable job"; "That Linda can get through her sadness over the end of her relationship with Austin." This final movement celebrates not only God's investment in the minutia of my life but also that I never walk the spiritual journey as a solitary pilgrim, disconnected from my relationships with family and friends.

Visio Divina

A method of prayer enjoyed by those who enjoy religious art, such as paintings, statuary, and icons, is called *visio divina* ("sacred seeing"). In her second letter to Agnes of Prague, the thirteenth-century Franciscan Clare of Assisi offered some advice about how to look upon the body of Jesus on a crucifix. She wrote, "Gaze on him, consider him, contemplate him, as you desire to imitate him." That provides a four-step method of meditation on religious art.

- Begin this method by *gazing* upon the figures depicted in the artwork. Notice their details. What are the expressions on their faces, their gestures, the composition's symmetry or lack of it, the interplay of light and shadows, and other artistic details? What are they suggesting?

- After having studied the portrayal of the scene or person(s), *consider* the motivation and intention of the artist. What message is the artist trying to convey? How does the artist express this meaning? What is striking about this depiction? What is missing or added to the customary depiction of this scene or person?

- As one ponders the answers to these questions, one grows silent as the message of the artwork emerges. This leads to *contemplation*, basking in the artist's visual representation of the scriptural passage or personage.

- This concludes with a deeper desire to *imitate* the Christlike qualities or virtues associated with the artwork's message.

Like artists who are challenged to find their own unique way to paint their subjects, we are challenged to find a way to be attentive and respond to God's invitations and requests in our lives. That attention and prayerfulness find expression in communal and private prayer. Our prayer techniques should aid us in opening the door of the heart to a God who yearns to enter more deeply within and transform us into instruments of peace, love, and justice.

REFLECTION QUESTIONS

1. On a scale of 1 (very dissatisfying) to 4 (very satisfying), how satisfying is communal prayer to me? What hinders or distracts me from fully engaging with it? What helps me to fully engage with it?

2. Which methods of scriptural prayer have been helpful to me? Which ones have been dissatisfying?

3. Google Caravaggio's paintings *The Taking of Christ, The Conversion of Saint Paul,* or *The Calling of Saint Matthew.* Practice *visio divina* with one of them. What reflections or emotions arose within me?

3

PRAYING RIGHT HERE

I pray from where I am and not from
where I think I should be.

"God, it's me, chatty Kathy,'" Kathleen said when I asked her how she prayed. "And then I tell God how happy I am for sending Joe into my life. The past twelve years of marriage have been pure bliss. And I thank God for little Joseph and Alice. Parenting them has been so fulfilling, and I let God know how grateful I am. Sometimes I let him know how delighted I am that Joe and I can make ends meet and have no financial burdens. 'You're such an awesome God! I just don't know how to give you adequate thanks and praise,' I'll sometimes say. And then I just sit there in stunned awe and gratitude."

I was delighted to hear about Kathleen's prayer method. She seems to know that prayer is partly about opening the door of the heart and expressing what's stored inside. It's about being honest and transparent and realizing that God wants us to open the door even wider to his unconditional love, care, and concern.

"

If there's a problem or issue for you in life, I guarantee you it's a problem or issue for God. God wants us to open our hearts to him and place every aspect of our lives into his hands.

"

Jackson's Experience

For Jackson, on the other hand, there was a time when prayer wasn't a positive experience. More accurately, it couldn't even happen.

"I am so angry with my brother-in-law. I can't even pray."

"What do you mean?" I asked.

"Last week, during our Thanksgiving meal, he said something about my sister that is not only a lie but also inappropriate to say in front of the family. I was shocked when I heard it. I spent the rest of the day just seething. And when I went to pray that evening, I realized I was blinded with anger and rage. I tried to find a proper place inside myself where I could ignore my feelings and just focus on God. But I couldn't. And I still can't."

When I pressed him, it was obvious Jackson believed that God wanted to hear only words of praise, adoration, and gratitude. Jackson even went so far as to say, "God wants us on our best behavior when we pray."

Have you ever found yourself thinking that? Have you ever found yourself wanting to do your usual mental "dance routine for Jesus," as I call it, but you can't find the appropriate music because some intrusive emotion with two left feet has chosen you as its dance partner?

"One challenge in prayer, Jackson," I countered, "is to pray from where we are and not from where we think we should be. That means being open, honest, and transparent with God. If there's a problem or issue for you in life, I guarantee you it's a problem or issue for God. God wants us to open our hearts to him and place every aspect of our lives into his hands. God wants to hear it all—the good, the bad, and the ugly."

"Even the anger toward my brother-in-law?"

"Yes, even that anger. No feeling or emotion is inappropriate to bring to God. Like I said, God wants to hear it all."

"But God knows everything," Jackson stated. "Doesn't he already see the anger in my heart? Why waste my time and his telling him what he already knows?"

I explained to Jackson that sharing feelings and experiences helps to build a long-lasting relationship. "That's how we fall in love with God. By opening our hearts to him, we discover he's eager to find a place to dwell even in a heart that is angry, sad, confused, forgotten, or forlorn. Once inside, he sometimes responds to our struggles and challenges," I added.

"How does he do that? How do I know God is talking to me?" Jackson asked.

I told him that by sharing our struggles and those emotions and feelings we think are inappropriate, we gain deeper insights into ourselves. Insights into our sinful behavior or judgmental attitudes are God's way of teaching us about ourselves and others. And sometimes we experience an emotional shift. We begin to see the situation in a whole new light and our perspective changes. We become more accepting and receptive to a personality trait, a particular person, or an event. And sometimes we might even get a nudge from God to reach out to someone, make a phone call, or send an email or text.

Six weeks later, Jackson returned for his spiritual direction session. I was delighted to see his change of attitude.

"I took your advice, Father. For almost three days straight, my entire prayer time consisted of my telling God just how angry and upset I was with my brother-in-law. I seemed to be stuck in the anger and just kept repeating myself over and over," Jackson said. He continued, "But then it dawned on me: Marie and Marty have been married for fifteen years. I'm sure Marty has seen sides of Marie that I am totally oblivious to. If they have issues between themselves, it's for them to sort out. I'm not a marriage counselor, and it's certainly not my role to interfere in their relationship. I never would have realized any of that if I hadn't spent time telling God how angry I was."

The Prayer of the Heart

Jackson's initial hesitancy to express his anger in prayer was simply another reminder to me how we so often live in our heads and are unwilling to tell God what's in our hearts. Though living in our heads with knowledge of God and his ways is important for our spiritual lives, it is ultimately unsatisfying: it promotes information, not intimacy. To be touched by God, we need to be vulnerable and open the door of the heart to him. We need to pray from the neck down.

Jesus knew this secret to intimacy and modeled the prayer of the heart time and again. He did not hesitate to open the door of his heart and express a wide range of emotions both to God and to others:

- After spending three days with people who had brought him the lame, blind, crippled, and mute to be healed, Jesus felt the hunger of the people and expressed his compassion for their predicament (see Matthew 15:32).

- His zeal for the sacredness of his Father's Temple was expressed by angrily overturning the tables of money changers, scattering their coins, and using a whip to drive out sheep, cattle, and doves for sale (see John 2:17).

- Matthew records Jesus praying a prayer of surprise to God at the lack of repentance in Chorazin, Bethsaida, and Capernaum, and a prayer of thanksgiving for revealing hidden things to little children (see Matthew 11:25-30).

- Jesus' disgust with the hypocrisy of the scribes and Pharisees is summed up in his calling them "snakes" and a "brood of vipers" (Matthew 23:33).

- The fourth Gospel mentions his love for Martha, her sister, and Lazarus (see John 11:5), being deeply moved in spirit and troubled by the grief of Mary and the Jews who followed her (see John 11:33), and weeping in sorrow at Lazarus' tomb (see John 11:35).

- Jesus was overwhelmed with grief in the garden of Gethsemane and expressed it to Peter, James, and John (see Matthew 26:38).

- In Luke's Gospel, we witness his evening anguish and hear his prayer to the Father as he struggled to surrender and accept the sacrifice of his life (see Luke 22:39-46).

These incidents remind us that emotions of their very nature, as Jesus instinctively knew, must be emoted. In themselves, emotions are neutral. It's how they are expressed that raises the possibility of sin. The challenge is to express them in appropriate and healthy ways. Kathleen shows us that positive feelings and emotions such as joy, love, hope, gratitude, and thanksgiving are eagerly shared with God and others. It's the negative feelings such as shame, anger, fear, nervousness, and confusion, as Jackson prompts us to consider, that we unfortunately treat as intrusions that must be repressed and buried. We mistakenly think that they should not be revealed to God or others. Consequently, they go underground and wreak havoc on us in unhealthy, passively aggressive ways: high blood pressure, headaches, muscle tension, ulcers, sleep disorders, binge eating or drinking, uncontrollable fits of anger, apathy, sarcasm, and inappropriate sexual behavior. Intimacy with God requires the same technique as intimacy with others: opening the door of the heart in vulnerability and sharing what we harbor within in an appropriate, honest way. The prayer of the heart is about praying from the neck down.

The Welcoming Prayer

How do we pray with those intrusive feelings that we deem inappropriate to express to God? How do we pray the prayer of the heart, from the neck down? There are four helpful spiritual practices.

The Welcoming Prayer, made popular some twenty-five years ago, offers one way to open the door of the heart and release our uncomfortable feelings and emotions. It consists of four simple steps: focus and sink in, name, welcome, let go.

- The first step is to focus on the unsettling emotion and feel it as a sensation in the body. How does it manifest itself physically? A tightened stomach? Sweaty palms? Tears? A frown on the face? A clenched jaw? A lump in the throat? A vengeful adrenaline surge? Tension in the shoulders? Allow yourself to fully experience the physical manifestation of the feeling.

- Once that is done, attempt to name this intrusive emotion. Is it anger or rage? Shame or guilt? Loneliness or solitary fatigue? Sexual desire or a lack of intimacy? Disappointment or discouragement? Sadness or depression? Take your time with this step and name it as accurately as you can in the present moment. Acknowledging the physicality of an emotion and naming it are signs of respect for its presence and power.

- The third step is to show hospitality to the emotion. "Welcome, fear." "Welcome, guilt." "Glad to see you, anger." "Welcome, loneliness." Don't judge the feeling or criticize its presence. Treat it as an honored guest that you are eager to get to know. This is how a negative emotion is befriended. Many people find it helpful to slowly repeat the greeting for a couple of minutes as they continue to feel the emotion's sensation.

- Once you have fully experienced, named, and embraced the emotion, slowly bid it farewell as the final step. Don't be tempted to rush this step or suppress this uncomfortable emotion. Take your time. I sometimes speak to the emotion directly and say, "Thanks for visiting me. You've taught me something. Goodbye." I am often pleasantly surprised at how an uncomfortable emotion slips away once it has been befriended and honored.

"Come as You Are" Prayer

"That doesn't seem like prayer to me," Philip objected when I taught him the Welcoming Prayer. "It seems more like a psychological technique."

Philip's point is well taken. Perhaps calling it a prayer is a misnomer. The purpose of this technique is to make us open, receptive, and comfortable with the uncomfortable emotions we experience on a day-to-day basis. We learn to pray *with* them, not *around* them. By welcoming them instead of stopping and stuffing them, we can learn to share them appropriately—with God and with others.

Alice designed a follow-up to the Welcoming Prayer. "I practice the Welcoming Prayer on a regular basis," she told me. "It helps me get in touch with some raw feelings, their bodily sensations, and how I sometimes am tempted to repress them. It also provides great preparation for what I call my 'Come as You Are' Prayer." She continued, "I start with a few minutes of silence. I remind myself that I am in the presence of God. I then survey my body and see what emotions it is registering. And then, using your image of opening the door of the heart, Fr. Albert, I share my feelings with God. I might tell God how angry I am at a friend's betrayal. Or maybe how alone and disconnected I am from my family and friends in Canada. I recently told him how frightened and nervous I was about an upcoming nursing examination. I also mentioned how sad and depressed I was at the loss of a boyfriend. It never ceases to amaze me how close and invested God is in my life when I take the time to tell him how I feel."

I instantly saw that the Welcoming Prayer followed by Alice's "Come as You Are" Prayer made for a wise combination. Befriending our intrusive, uncomfortable emotions and then telling God about them not only make our prayer authentic and transparent but also provide balm for a headache, a heartache, or a bruised or battered soul.

The Psalms

There's a third prayer method that is helpful for expressing any emotion, be it intrusive, intense, or inspirational.

The 150 psalms found in the Book of Psalms are ancient religious hymns composed over five centuries and likely used during worship in the Temple of Jerusalem. Some are also associated with the royal court. To this day, they are sung and prayed in synagogues and churches. Contemporary clergy, religious, and some laity, both communally and individually, embrace them daily in praying the Liturgy of the Hours ("the breviary").

The genius of praying the psalms is twofold.

First, it can enlarge our personal experience and connect it with millions of others who have lived before us. Praying them allows us to weave our private, twenty-first-century story into the rich tapestry of humanity's salvation history. As Amy prays Psalm 23, she reflects upon God's loving care for her and how God shepherds her just as he did with the chosen people in the Exodus. In a moment of distress, Aiden prayed Psalm 22 with Jesus as the opening verses captured his feeling of abandonment:

> My God, my God, why have you forsaken me?
>   Why are you so far from helping me, from the words
>   of my groaning?

> O my God, I cry by day, but you do not answer;
>> and by night, but find no rest. (22:1-2)

Second, as one becomes familiar with the psalms, one can see that they give voice to just about every human emotion—both the rowdy and the raw. I remember once complaining to my spiritual director that God was sleeping on the job and not answering a petition I had been placing before him for over a month.

"There's a psalm for that!" my director exclaimed. He opened the Bible at his side and gave voice to the final four verses of Psalm 44:

> Rouse yourself! Why do you sleep, O Lord?
>> Awake, do not cast us off forever!
> Why do you hide your face?
>> Why do you forget our affliction and oppression?
> For we sink down to the dust;
>> our bodies cling to the ground.
> Rise up, come to our help.
>> Redeem us for the sake of your steadfast love. (44:23-26)

Ever felt so livid that you momentarily wished harm upon what your perceived enemies hold most dear? The psalmist surely did. Remembering the Edomites and Babylonians, who were old enemies of Jerusalem, the psalmist sang:

> Remember, O Lord, against the Edomites
>> the day of Jerusalem's fall,
> how they said, "Tear it down! Tear it down!
>> Down to its foundations!"
> O daughter Babylon, you devastator!
>> Happy shall they be who pay you back
>> what you have done to us!

> Happy shall they be who take your little ones
> and dash them against the rock! (137:7-9)

The psalms also celebrate God as the Creator who is to be adored as we sit, rapt in awe and wonder (Psalms 8, 9, 19, 29, 48). They are prayers we pray in times of distress, trauma, and loss (Psalms 3, 6, 12, 13, 31, 69, 70). Psalms 78 and 105 express gratitude for God's grace. Some psalms are thankful for God's action, answered petitions, and deliverance (Psalms 16, 18, 40, 92, 107, 124). Others sing of confidence, trust, and faith in God (Psalms 11, 23, 27). They even give advice for living in relationship with God (Psalms 1, 49, 119). Psalm 51 is perfect to pray when we are weighed down by the guilt of our sins or as we prepare for the Sacrament of Reconciliation.

I always encourage my spiritual directees to become acquainted with the Book of Psalms. I invite them to read a psalm a day. Some directees choose one at random; Charlie, on the other hand, prays them in order, starting with Psalm 1, and is currently up to Psalm 88. Before my directees pray a particular psalm, I suggest they note the title given by the translators and read the footnotes associated with the psalm they have chosen. As they become familiar with various psalms, they discover which ones might fit their differing moods. And with that discovery, they find themselves opening the door of the heart to God and expressing some emotions that they previously might have considered intrusive and inappropriate to mention to God.

The Stations of the Cross

The practice of following the fourteen Stations of the Cross, begun in fifth-century Italy but made popular by the Franciscans in the fifteenth and sixteenth centuries, is a traditional way of following Jesus as he walks the *Via Dolorosa* to Calvary. At each station, we pause and ponder his reaction as he is condemned to death, takes up his cross, falls three times, encounters his mother and Veronica and the women of Jerusalem, is helped by Simon of Cyrene, is stripped of his garments, dies, and is taken down from the cross and buried. The goal of this spiritual practice is to walk with Jesus and compassionately marvel at the depths of his sacrificial love.

Sandra surprised me with her practice of this devotion. "I pray the Stations of the Cross whenever I feel overwhelmed by a cacophony of emotions elicited by a single incident. Or when I feel unjustly accused, stripped of my dignity and reputation, and a failure all at the same time. I think of Simon of Cyrene when I resent being coerced into helping someone at work, or of Jesus when I feel abandoned by friends. I take these feelings—confusion, resentment, failure, discouragement, despondency, grief, and sorrow—and unite them with Jesus's experience as he walks to Calvary. The Stations give a voice to the raw emotions I sometimes struggle to articulate."

When we are not our best selves, it's so tempting to shut the door of the heart to God and hide. We think that God isn't interested in us when we are feeling unsettling emotions that we believe shouldn't be brought into the light. So we hide in our heads, praying from where we think we should be, instead of where we actually are. Spiritual practices such as the Welcoming Prayer followed by the Come as You Are Prayer, the Psalms, and the Stations of the Cross challenge such thinking and remind us that one of the greatest gifts we can give to God is to open the door of the heart and invite him to sit in the messiness of our lives.

Reflection Questions

1. What are the most common emotions and feelings that I express to God in prayer? What are the least common?

2. When do I feel hesitant, leery, wary, or uncomfortable praying from where I am? What does this say about my relationship with God?

3. What spiritual practices keep me open, honest, and transparent with God? How could they help in my openness and honesty with others?

4

PETITIONING AND INTERCEDING

I petition God and intercede for others as expressions
of my care, concern, and compassion. I do not try to
convince or coax a change in God's will.

Thirty-year-old Jo Marie was discerning a religious vocation to a cloistered community of nuns. She had discovered the Carmelites and was
intrigued by their dedication to prayer.

Knowing that every cloistered community has its own unique characteristics, I suggested she investigate the Poor Clares as an alternative point
of comparison.

"I don't know where there's a Poor Clare monastery," she told me.

"I do. I'm very close to the Poor Clares in Memphis. Let me telephone
the abbess of the monastery and see if it's possible for you to spend some
time with them," I said.

After our spiritual direction session ended, I called my good friend Sr.
Marguerite. I arranged for Jo Marie to spend a week with the Memphis Poor
Clares. She would live in the cloister, eat and pray with the sisters, and help
with the daily chores of the monastery. Jo Marie was just as excited receiving the news as I was to give it.

I anxiously awaited Jo Marie's return from Memphis and our next spiritual direction session. I was curious to hear her impression of these wonderful nuns.

"What did you think?" I asked Jo Marie after we sat down and said a brief prayer.

"Fr. Albert, to be honest, I was very disappointed. Those nuns weren't really cloistered. I could tell by the petitions at daily Mass as well as the intercessions at morning and evening prayers, they knew more about what was going on in the world than I did."

I explained to Jo Marie that the spiritual life is not simply about "me and God," and one does not enter the cloister to leave the world. Rather, the spiritual life is a family affair, and one enters the cloister to be inserted more deeply into the world with its turmoil, tribulations, and trials. A cloistered contemplative intercedes to God for the world. To authentically open the door of the heart to God, one must also open the windows of the soul to the world. Otherwise, one is inviting God into a walk-in freezer.

Praying the News

My friendship with the Memphis Poor Clares started years ago, when I was asked to preach a weeklong retreat to them. I remember the day I discovered an innovative way to pray.

During a day of Eucharistic adoration, I went into the chapel and was taken aback to see Sr. Angela sitting before the Blessed Sacrament and reading the newspaper! "What is going on here?" I asked myself with surprise and dismay.

The following morning, I was in the sacristy preparing for Mass. Sr. Marguerite entered and asked me if I had everything I needed. I told her that I did and thanked her.

"Can I ask you something?" I gingerly whispered before she left.

"Certainly."

I told her how the day before, I had entered the chapel and was surprised to see one of the nuns—I chose not to mention Sr. Angela by name—reading the newspaper before the Blessed Sacrament. The abbess must have heard the confusion and surprise in my voice.

"Oh, Albert," she said, "don't let it affect your blood pressure. That was Sr. Angela." (I took undue delight that she knew the culprit!) "She likes to pray the news. That's how she discovered her vocation within her vocation."

"Praying the news? Her vocation within her vocation?" I asked with my head cocked.

"Yes, as she reads different stories in the newspaper, she ponders in her heart if God is calling her to respond in some way. A few years ago, while praying over the news, Sr. Angela was deeply affected by the high rate of teenage suicides. She felt called to do something about it. So now, whenever she reads about a teenager dying by his or her own hand, she writes a short note of sympathy to the family, sends it to the funeral home, and asks the funeral home to pass it along to the family."

Sr. Angela had discovered a unique and avant-garde way to pray. Her technique demonstrates another way how God, like the persistent widow found in Jesus' parable (see Luke 18:1-5), knocks on the door of the heart (see Revelation 3:20). If some local, national, or international news touches us, that might well be the God of surprise and disguise calling us to compassionately open the heart's door to the hungry, the thirsty, the stranger, the naked, the sick, or those in prison (see Matthew 25:31-46). We can respond with the prayer of intercession or by giving a donation or writing a note or learning about the back story of the situation. Sr. Angela's method is a vivid reminder that we never walk alone with God on the spiritual journey, that we must always keep the windows of the soul open to the world, and that our prayerfulness should always lead to action.

The World Mission Rosary

Priest, bishop, and later archbishop Fulton J. Sheen offered a prayer technique that helps to keep the windows of the soul open to the world. Author of seventy-three books and referred to as "the first televangelist" by *Time* magazine in April 1952 because of his immensely popular radio and subsequent television programs, Sheen was also the national director of the Society for the Propagation of the Faith. In February 1951, during his radio show *The Catholic Hour*, he told his listeners that they must pray not only for themselves but also for the world. "To this end, I have designed the World Mission Rosary," he said.

Like any other rosary, the World Mission Rosary consists of five decades. Each decade, however, is a different color and represents one of the five populated continents:

- The blue of sapphire represents the countries and islands in the Blue Pacific, thus Australia and Oceana.

- The green of emerald symbolizes the green forests and jungles of Africa.

- The white of crystal symbolizes Europe, the home of the Pope, and the spiritual capital of early Christianity.

- The yellow of topaz represents all Asian countries and the Middle East, where the sun first rises, and civilization first began.

- The red of ruby represents the Americas, Latin America, the United States, and Canada, first inhabited by the Native Americans and First Nations people.

"When the Rosary is finished, the person has embraced all continents, all people in prayer," Sheen concluded. A person tours the world by praying the World Mission Rosary.

Unable to fulfill his dream of being a missionary to a foreign land because of health issues, Aaron finds the World Mission Rosary extraordinarily attractive and has enthusiastically embraced it. Over the past three years, this Rosary has led him to research each of the continents to discover specific intentions for which he prays. As he prays the blue decade, he petitions God that the Australian government would begin to address the significant overrepresentation of First Nations people in the criminal justice system and the cruel treatment of asylum seekers. The green decade gets him praying for the end of violent extremism and terrorism that plague many African countries. The white decade that represents Europe gets Aaron reflecting on climate change and an aging population that some scholars consider to be the most pressing issues for the European Union. The yellow decade has Aaron interceding for ethnic and religious minorities persecuted by some repressive Asian countries. The red decade has him praying for an end to gun violence in America. The World Mission Rosary is a daily reminder to Aaron to keep the windows of his soul wide open.

Making a Difference?

As he continues to research the turmoil and trials of the five populated continents and intercedes to God for them, Aaron sometimes wonders if God is hearing his prayer. And if God is hearing his prayer, why doesn't God respond?

Ever wonder, like Aaron, if God is listening to your prayer? Why doesn't God answer your petitions? I've had the same questions time and again. They usually arise over a specific intention for which I am praying.

As a young Franciscan friar, I still remember getting a phone call from the wife of one of my best friends from high school. She told me that her husband, Paul, had been diagnosed with brain cancer. "It doesn't look good," she whispered over the phone. The phone call didn't last long. Hanging up

"

WE'LL NEVER BE ABLE
TO UNDERSTAND
THE WAYS OF GOD. ALL
WE CAN DO IS BOW BEFORE
GOD, SURRENDER, AND
TRUST. THAT'S PROBABLY THE
MOST DIFFICULT PRACTICE IN
THE SPIRITUAL LIFE.

"

the phone, I was saddened and in shock. But I was convinced that fervent prayer could gain a healing for Paul. So I made it a point to begin praying for his healing at daily Mass and at morning and evening prayers.

Two months later, Lisa called me again. "Paul died peacefully in his sleep last night." I didn't know what to say. She told me that someone would give me a follow-up phone call with the funeral arrangements.

I made an appointment to see my spiritual director.

"What did I do wrong? Was I supposed to be praying in a different way? Why didn't God answer my prayer? Why would God take a married man in his late twenties with a two-year-old daughter?" I blabbered these questions as I tried to get in touch with my feelings and understand why God chose not to answer my prayer—or, more accurately, flatly refused my request.

"There're no adequate answers to those questions, Albert," Fr. Robb said. "God is a mystery of infinite, unconditional love at the root of our existence. As a mystery, we'll never be able to understand the ways of God. All we can do is bow before God, surrender, and trust. That's probably the most difficult practice in the spiritual life.

"But I can tell you, your prayer was not wasted. It softened your heart and made it more tender and compassionate. No doubt Paul's wife found consolation in knowing that her husband's best friend was praying for him. Your prayers assured her that she wasn't going through this experience alone. That must have given her daily strength. You were expanding her idea of family.

"And don't think you could have prayed in a different or more successful way. Prayer is not a magic wand that we wave, while saying the magic word *abracadabra* and pulling a rabbit out of a hat. Nor is it a rain dance that, when done properly, makes the skies open up and rain come down. And it isn't some technique we use to twist God's arm and force God to accommodate himself to our will.

"When all is said and done, we petition and intercede to expand the size of our hearts and to affirm our connection with the wider family of the world. And in doing that, we come to a place where we can bow before God, surrender, and trust in his providence."

Jesus' Teaching

During my theology training for ordination to the priesthood, I discovered Jesus had offered similar advice about trusting in God's response to our prayers.

In the eleventh chapter of Luke's Gospel, Jesus tells a parable, found only in the third Gospel, about a man who approaches his friend at midnight with the request for three loaves of bread for a visitor. His friend refuses, saying the door is locked and his children are in bed. But some scholars say the text implies the petitioner keeps knocking. Jesus notes, "I tell you, even though he will not get up and give him anything because he is his friend, at least because of his persistence he will get up and give him whatever he needs" (Luke 11:8).

The rare Greek word *anaideia*, rendered here as "persistence," is a challenge to translate. It is found nowhere else in the New Testament. Because a first-century town's honor and reputation were based upon its hospitality, some scholars believe the word is better translated as "avoidance of shame" and refers to the friend in bed and not the neighbor in need. Hence, a better translation of the sentence would be "I tell you, even though he will not get up and give him anything because he is his friend, at least because he wants to avoid being shamed, he will get up and give him whatever he needs."

Jesus' commentary on the parable supports this latter translation:

"So I say to you, Ask, and it will be given you; search, and you will find; knock, and the door will be opened for you. For everyone who asks receives, and everyone who searches finds, and for everyone who knocks, the door will be opened. Is there anyone among you who, if your child asks for a fish, will give a snake instead of a fish? Or if the child asks for an egg, will give a scorpion? If you then, who are evil, know how to give good gifts to your children, how much more will the heavenly Father give the Holy Spirit to those who ask him!" (Luke 11:9-13)

Jesus uses a rhetorical technique of deduction in his commentary where something that applies in a lesser case must also apply in a more important one: our heavenly Father will outdo the response of any parent. In doing so, he is making three important points about petitions and intercessions.

- The grammatical forms of the Greek verbs are better translated "Keep on asking . . . seeking . . . knocking." Because the verbs lack specific direct objects, Jesus is not teaching *what* to pray for but *how* to pray—with tenacity, trust, and persistence.

- Jesus is not suggesting that God will *grant* every petition or intercession. Rather, he is highlighting the fact that God will *respond*. One should trust in God's loving concern and providence. "To avoid being shamed," God will not deceive the petitioner or intercessor.

- Luke changes Matthew's gift of "good things" (Matthew 7:11) to "the Holy Spirit," thus highlighting the superabundant generosity of our heavenly Father.

The parable and its commentary celebrate a God who is more generous than an inconvenienced neighbor and more straightforward than a miserly, cruel parent. Though God seemingly delays responding or outright denies our petitions and intercessions—Aaron experiences God's silence to his worldwide petitions and my friend Paul died despite my prayers—Jesus challenges us to continue praying with tenacity and trust in God's care, concern, and compassion.

Why?

Sometimes our trust in God's concern can cause us to ask, "Why is God silent?" or "Why did God refuse my request?" Such questions can easily lead to logical, preposterous explanations that portray God as a cruel, tyrannical ogre who uses silence and refusal "to teach me to be patient" or "to build up my character" or "to purify me" or "to punish me for my past sins."

We fail to remember that wrestling with divine silence and refusal can lead us to a place where our own desires—with their accompanying petitions and intercessions—can be transformed. We come to a place of surrender and trust as we grapple with our personal demands. Persistent petitioning and interceding with no apparent divine response can change *our* minds, not God's. We begin to trust and think, "God has another way of dealing with this situation" or "God has other plans for this person."

The question to ask is not "Why?" but "How am I to respond? How do I maintain childlike trust when the silence of God is deafening or his reply is negative and definitive? How do I stay in a relationship with God when I feel cynical, resentful, or skeptical of his response?"

Irene's Response

Several years ago, a spiritual directee taught me her method of maintaining trust and staying in a relationship with God when she didn't receive the requested answer to a petition or intercession. "Sometimes, Father, odd as it sounds, we have to forgive God," Irene said.

I have used Irene's technique on several occasions. It consists of four simple steps.

- Begin by calling to mind the presence of God that surrounds us like the air we breathe. This divine presence is a loving, compassionate mystery. We can never understand or fathom the depths of this mystery of love. All we can do is bow before it.

- Second, bring the person or situation for whom we are petitioning and interceding to mind. Do not analyze or try to find meaning in God's silence or response to this person or situation. Just sit in God's presence and place the person or situation in the hands of God.

- After a few minutes, take a breath. As you inhale, accept God's response. You might want to say to yourself, "Acceptance." Think of Jesus in the garden of Gethsemane as he prayed, "Not my will but yours be done" (Luke 22:42).

- As you exhale, submit to God's will. You might want to say to yourself, "Surrender." Think of Jesus' last moments from the cross as he prayed, "Father, into your hands I commend my spirit" (Luke 23:46).

Practice these four steps for a few minutes before concluding with the Lord's Prayer.

Irene's simple method of "forgiving God," when done often, breeds a deep trust in God's care, concern, and compassion for the challenges and sufferings of this world.

It's such a temptation to think that we are solitaries on the spiritual journey. But we are not. We walk together in a pilgrim Church with others who, like ourselves, have their own struggles and difficulties. As we open the door of the heart to God, we open the windows of our soul to the world. In doing so, we live the two great commandments of loving God and loving our neighbor (see Mark 12:30-31).

REFLECTION QUESTIONS

1. On a scale of 1 (not at all) to 4 (very), how knowledgeable am I of local, national, and international news? How often does that knowledge play a role in my daily prayers of petition and intercession?

2. In the past, how have I explained or made sense of God's silence or refusal to answer my prayers? Did I think God was stretching, testing, or punishing me? Why?

3. In what current situations of my life might Irene's method of "forgiving God" prove helpful? Would I feel more comfortable calling it by a different name? Why?

5

TRYING TOO HARD

Frustration and burnout in prayer are signs that I am
trying too hard.

I was surprised to hear the number of spiritual practices forty-year-old Justin could cram into one day.

"My wife and I pray morning prayer and evening prayer from the breviary every day together. I like to pray the Divine Mercy chaplet while heading to and from work on the commuter train. During my hour-long lunch break at work, I try to finish eating in thirty minutes so I have time to pray the Rosary. And before heading to bed, I like to do some spiritual reading—either from Scripture or a contemporary book—for about thirty minutes or so. On weekends, I typically pray a second daily Rosary."

Chuckling, I said, "I'm exhausted just hearing you do all that in a single day," and asked, "Why so many spiritual practices?"

"I don't want God to forget me. And I believe this will help me get more of God's attention and love," Justin responded.

Four months later, I wasn't surprised to hear that Justin had abandoned most of those daily spiritual practices. "I need to take a break and breathe," he whispered with a vacant stare.

"

OUR DEEPENING
SENSITIVITY TO
GOD CAN OCCUR NOT
ONLY THROUGH FORMAL
PERIODS OF PRAYER BUT
ALSO THROUGH ANY
ACTIVITY THAT PROMOTES
SELF-REFLECTION AND
GODLY ATTENTION.

"

Nothing to Get

Ever find yourself overcommitted to daily spiritual practices? Ever feel like spiritually you have bitten off more than you can chew? Ever feel worn out, like Justin, with an overzealous approach to the life of prayer or a super-sized menu of spiritual practices that need to be completed?

Many beginners live with the misconception that people can "get more God," as Julie once told me, the more they fill their day with spiritual practices. "The more you pray, the more you get in return," she said.

Nothing could be further from the truth. God and grace are not commodities that we can purchase with our prayer. Nor can we force God's presence with a snap of the fingers or the folding of hands. We don't "get more God" or earn more of God's love and attention by spending more time in prayer.

In the Sermon on the Mount, Jesus himself hints to this misconception, found in many beginners in the spiritual life, when he teaches, "When you are praying, do not heap up empty phrases as the Gentiles do; for they think that they will be heard because of their many words. Do not be like them, for your Father knows what you need before you ask him" (Matthew 6:7-8). The purpose of prayer is to make us prayerful—that is, sensitive to the God of surprise and disguise who surrounds us like the air we breathe and knocks on the door of the heart in the nitty-gritty of our daily lives.

There's nothing to "get" in the spiritual life because we already have it. We simply need to become more aware of how God, persistently knocking on the door of our hearts, asks us to help foster the kingdom with acts of peace, love, and justice. That deepening sensitivity can occur not only through formal periods of prayer but also through any activity that promotes self-reflection and godly attention. Some of these activities include the following:

- gardening;

- flower arranging;

- walking or jogging;

- working on a craft;

- observing nature—bees, birds, butterflies, caterpillars, clouds, the night sky—closely;

- sipping morning coffee or tea on the back porch or in the kitchen;

- walking hand-in-hand with someone on the beach;

- journaling;

- cooking a meal;

- folding clothes;

- looking out the window of a bus, commuter train, or plane;

- sitting in your favorite chair, closing your eyes, and reflecting on your day;

- layering frosting on a newly baked cake;

- scrolling through photographs and enjoying the memories they generate;

- doing the dishes by hand.

One way of overcoming spiritual frustration and burnout is to understand the potential of such simple activities as helpful and expressive of your spirituality. You don't have to practice explicitly *spiritual* activities to be spiritual. You simply need to open the door of the heart and be attentive to God not only in the myriad divine manifestations but also in what God is asking of you. Fostering the continual intention to be reflective and prayerful is more important than any specific technique practiced for a set time.

The Well Runs Dry

Unlike Justin's, Aiden's dilemma wasn't an overcommitment to spiritual practices. After making the commitment to daily prayer for about six months, he experienced a typical turning point in the spiritual journey.

"I really have grown to love prayer. It really hasn't challenged or disrupted my daily schedule the way I thought it might. It has become part of my daily routine, and I look forward to it. It brings me so much peace and joy. Those emotions are palpable and feel like refreshing water welling up from a well deep inside me. A couple of weeks ago, I even said to myself, 'I must remember how I got here. It's a good place for me to return to tomorrow.'

"The following day, those emotions suddenly dried up. I didn't feel anything. I was so annoyed because I searched and searched for that special inner space and couldn't find it. It disappeared. I tried my best to pump up some feelings of peace and joy, but they weren't coming. It was as if the well had run dry. And it remains dry. It's been three weeks, and I don't understand what I'm doing wrong. How do I rediscover that place of peace and joy?"

Aiden's loss of the emotional consolations that prayer sometimes provides is really an important turning point in his prayer life. I'll discuss it in the next chapter. For now, let me offer three reminders about his frantic and frustrated search for the well of peace and joy.

The first is to never confuse the gifts with the Giver. It's so tempting to equate the feelings of peace and joy—or any emotion for that matter—with God. God is not an emotion but a presence. Sometimes God's presence will bring us warm, gratifying feelings like peace and joy, as does the presence of any friend or spouse. But also like the presence of any friend or spouse, that doesn't always happen. Nor should it. God is so much more and beyond any human emotion we might experience within the confines of our physical bodies.

Second, prayer is not a fire hydrant of satisfying emotions that we can turn on or off at will. And it's ill-advised to manufacture uplifting feelings. "It's so tempting," I told Aiden, "to think of prayer as the medicine to take for relief from a headache or heartache. It's true that sometimes we do find solace and consolation in our prayer. But sometimes we do not. One of the classic definitions of prayer and contemplation is "a long, loving look at the Real."[1] So all we can do is sit where we find ourselves and ponder how to open the door of the heart more widely to the God of surprise and disguise in this present moment. At times, that will feel like opening the door to a desert, wasteland, or wilderness. But even in that desert or wasteland, God can speak to our hearts. Through the prophet Hosea, God said, 'Therefore, I will now allure her, and bring her into the wilderness, and speak tenderly to her' (2:14)."

Third, personal expectations are the bane of prayer. As in any other relationship with a friend or spouse, they can be the cause of disappointment and discouragement as we try to force or manipulate gifts from the Giver. We do not pray to get anything. We spend time with God, as we do in the other important relationships we nurture, so we can open the door of the heart ever wider and eagerly respond to any divine invitation or request.

Discouragement

In my mid-twenties, I experienced a different kind of discontent and discouragement with my spiritual life.

"I've been praying daily for an hour for over ten years," I told my spiritual director. "After all this time, I think I should be further along on the spiritual journey. But I'm still getting distracted in prayer. I grow tired and weary of trying to fight off the distractions—and when I do, they keep returning. So I typically just give in to them.

"I go through dry periods when nothing seems to be happening, and I end up pondering the clock more than the crucifix. I feel stuck—or maybe like I am going backward—or maybe even failing. I'm frustrated and just don't know how to get to the next stage of the spiritual journey. I feel drained and stressed out by trying harder and harder and making no progress."

When I sat back and listened to what I had just said, it dawned on me that perhaps I wasn't the problem. My spiritual director was. Maybe he didn't know how to direct me to the next level of spiritual maturity. Though he was my second director in as many as eight months, maybe I had chosen wrongly or already outgrown him. Did he know how to help or accompany me? Perhaps I needed to start looking for yet another spiritual director.

That period in my life was not unique to me. Over the years, I've heard similar complaints time and again from people with whom I have accompanied as a spiritual director. Those complaints are rooted in a few misconceptions that generate such discontent and discouragement with the life of prayer.

Any experienced cook will tell you, "A watched pot never boils." The same can be said of the life of prayer. Some people are always studying, analyzing, and overthinking their progress in prayer. Such navel-gazing is most unhelpful when it comes to the spiritual journey. Fidelity to daily prayer will naturally lead to new vistas on the spiritual journey but those vistas are rarely front-and-center to our vision. We occasionally catch a fleeting sight of them with our peripheral vision, but, more typically, we see them only in hindsight. It is a misconception to think that growth in prayer is immediately discernible and detectable from yesterday's or yester-year's stage. Heightened sensitivity to the presence of God, which is the immediate goal of prayer, occurs intermittently and incrementally over a lifetime, not instantaneously and immediately over a day, month, or year.

Thinking that progress in prayer can be attained by the sheer force of will is a second misconception. As my spiritual director wisely told me, "You are where you are because this is where God wants you to be. When God wants you further along on the spiritual journey, he'll come into your life, pick you up, and move you there. Until then, all you can do is remain faithful to your daily prayer and be content with God's grace. Fidelity to prayer is like buying a train ticket and standing on the platform. Only God decides when the train arrives to move you farther along the spiritual journey."

A third misconception suspects the existence of a secret recipe for spiritual growth. Or that a certain prayer technique, a particular spiritual writer, or even an experienced spiritual director is the microwave oven that will transform our prayer life within seconds. This is why, with the best of intentions, we go on a quixotic search for and gobble up books by a certain author or change spiritual directors willy-nilly. The life of prayer occurs in the crockpot of a lifetime, not in the microwave oven of a year or a decade with a certain author or a particular spiritual director serving as our cook.

Experienced pilgrims and their spiritual directors are always on the lookout for the presence of spiritual discontent and discouragement. When they find their hearts heavy and their heads hung low, they consider some helpful questions such as these:

- What is the misconception generating my disappointment, discontent, or discouragement?

- What unconscious or unspoken expectation is making me feel powerless and needy?

- Is this fatigue, stress, or disappointment a result of trying too hard or trying to force God's grace?

- Am I analyzing or overthinking my prayer life? Why?

- Why am I not content to be spiritually where God's grace has led me?

These are important questions to raise and address in a spiritual direction session. They help to unmask a potential temptation to lock the door of the heart and give up on prayer. When we give in to that temptation, we have fallen victim to the deadly sin of acedia, the deliberate decision to terminate any relationship with God.

The Prayer of Just Sitting

Ever find yourself fidgeting with a piece of jewelry like a wedding ring or fussing with your hair as you sit and pray? Ever find a cloud of nervousness, agitation, disinterest, or boredom hanging over your prayer time? During a prayer period, have you ever asked yourself in desperation, "Just what *am* I doing here?"

Such unsettled reactions are not as uncommon as you might think. Both beginners and seasoned pilgrims occasionally experience them during times of prayer. They are often indications that unconscious misconceptions and expectations still are lurking around and the temptation to use sheer brute force to advance prayer hasn't died.

There's a simple antidote to trying too hard in prayer that I recommend to my spiritual directees, both the beginner and the seasoned. It is based on the fact that growth in prayer is a result of God's grace. Just as fruit on a tree ripens not by its own effort but by sitting in the sun, so too we grow spiritually mature just by sitting in the light of God's presence. I call this simple technique the Prayer of Just Sitting. Just as I do, I suggest directees practice it periodically—once or twice a week—for fifteen minutes. It is not meant to be a replacement for my daily prayer routine. It's quite easy to practice.

- Begin by finding a comfortable chair and settling into it. If it's a recliner, you might want to stretch your legs. Take a few deep breaths. With your eyes closed, become aware of your body and what it's feeling. Do you have any aches or pains? Is your stomach growling? How are you feeling emotionally?

- Then move your awareness to your immediate surroundings. What are you hearing? Is the temperature comfortable? If there are any noticeable distractions, deal with them and then return to your chair and begin again.

- Imagine the light of God's grace shining upon you as if it were the sun and you were an apple. Just sit and bask in God's grace.

- Distracting thoughts will immediately assail you. Acknowledge them. "Hello, reminder-that-there-are-clothes-in-the-washing-machine-that-need-to-be-put-in-the-dryer. I'll respond to you in a few minutes. But for now, I'm going to just sit here." Consider again God's grace shining upon you.

- Another distraction will inevitably arise. "I see you, need-to-call-the-dentist-and-change-my-appointment. I'll take care of you later. But for now, I'm going to just sit here." Recall again God's light surrounding you.

- If you fear you will forget the message of the distraction, write it down on a piece of paper and then return to just sitting.

- Continue this practice for fifteen minutes. Acknowledge each distraction but then return to just sitting. When your timer goes off, conclude with the Our Father and the Sign of the Cross.

The practice of the Prayer of Just Sitting has but one goal: to consciously remind us that growth in prayer is not a result of the brute force of will or a personal achievement. It is a gradual grace from God as he knocks on the door of the heart and asks us to open it more widely to his request to help build the kingdom of peace, love, and justice.

Just as friends go out for a meal together and spouses build a life together, so too spiritual pilgrims build and nurture a relationship with God through prayer. The life of prayer can't be forced and often is riddled with unspoken expectations and unfortunate misconceptions. As prayer blossoms in our midst, we come to an ever-deepening realization that it is a grace and gift that can only be received by a heart whose door is opened.

REFLECTION QUESTIONS

1. What unspoken expectations and misconceptions have plagued my relationships in the past? How have I brought them into my relationship with God?

2. What have been the sources of my frustrations in prayer? When and why do I occasionally feel worn out by my prayer?

3. When have I been tempted to analyze and overthink my progress in prayer? Why? What need in me does that satisfy?

6

PRAYING BEYOND WORDS

Growth in prayer is moving from words to silence.

I still remember the joy I experienced as a fourteen-year-old who had made the commitment to daily prayer. Praying with various spiritual books was thought-provoking and satisfying. I looked forward to that hour every afternoon. I felt like I was making a lot of spiritual progress and, on occasion, proudly thought I was on my way to becoming a mystic.

But after six or seven months, everything changed. It became difficult to ponder and think about paragraphs. Praying with words over a paragraph or sentence long got in the way. It was as if this hour, once a source of satisfying spiritual nourishment, had dried up or turned rancid. I suspected I was going backward—or even worse, I had offended God in some way, and this was the natural consequence or punishment for my sin. I knew it was time to make another appointment with Fr. Murray so I could figure out what I was doing wrong.

"Welcome to the next stage of the journey," Fr. Murray said. He assured me I neither was going backward nor had offended God in some unknown way. I was experiencing an important turning point in my prayer. Though it certainly didn't seem like it, I was making progress.

From Kataphatic to Apophatic Prayer

Over the years, I have often returned to that memory as I sit with people in spiritual direction. Sooner or later, sometimes after four to seven months of daily prayer, I hear the same complaints from my directees: "Prayer is dissatisfying." "I'm bored to tears during my prayer time." "My progress has come to a screeching halt." "I'm no longer getting a spiritual buzz when I pray." Hearing these or similar complaints, I know it's time to offer a little teaching on the two main types of prayer.

Just about everyone begins their relationship with God leaning on *kataphatic* prayer. Kataphatic prayer uses the five senses, objects, and creation as a ladder to bring a person into the presence of God. A lighted candle, music like Gregorian chant or contemporary praise and worship music, a sunrise or sunset, the Rosary, burning incense, a Scripture passage or spiritual book, even a photo of the Alps can help people "raise the mind and heart to God,"[2] to quote the seventh-century saint John Damascene's classic definition of prayer. Words are the primary means of communication in kataphatic prayer. We're in control as we open the heart's door and express our thoughts and feelings to God. Kataphatic prayer is analogous to communication between friends or people who are starting to date. There are sensory consolations like peace and deep-seated joy that arise and keep a person returning to a daily prayer commitment. Spiritual progress is palpable.

Praying with Creation

Fr. Herb has a unique form of kataphatic prayer that has led him to a prayerful attitude. His various prayer methods, such as the Eucharist, the Liturgy of the Hours, an occasional Rosary, and *lectio divina*, have made him mindful and attentive to how God persistently knocks on the door of his heart. He also encounters the God of surprise and disguise when he works in the garden.

"I can easily spend the entire day in the garden," he once confessed to me. "Weeding around the cacti, watering the tomato plants, and tending the herbs lead me to an inner place where I get close to God."

"How so?" I asked.

"A few years ago, while preparing a Bible study on the Letter to the Romans, I was reminded that St. Paul discovered what I had discovered on my own. In the first chapter, he mentions how God's eternal power and divine nature, invisible as they are, can be understood and seen through creation (see Romans 1:20). I resonated with that because sometimes I use the cacti and the other plants as a way to experience God.

"As I weed and water, I become *aware* and focus my *attention* on an individual cactus plant, a ripening tomato, or the clump of chives. And then I *assess* how this plant, fruit, or herb reveals to me God's goodness, power, beauty, and presence. I might take notice of the subtle beauty of the frail cactus flower and how God has allowed it to flower just for my enjoyment. Or I become aware how God's love and care for my nourishment have pushed the tomato to flower from its vine and ripen for my enjoyment. I see God's hand in the chives and say a prayer of thanks and *adoration* for how they will taste in my homemade soup."

Speaking from his Franciscan roots, Fr. Herb smiled and told me, "St. Francis got it right in the Canticle of Creatures! You can use any part of creation—the sun, the moon, fire, water, the earth—to experience the majesty of God."

Living with Fr. Herb, I discovered that his kataphatic method of praying with creation—awareness, attention, assessment, and adoration—was something that he would return to time and again.

"

DRYNESS IS A SIGN THAT SOMETHING IS COOKING. YOU'RE ABOUT TO TURN A CORNER. FOLLOW THE SILENCE AND SIT IN IT.

"

A Rickety Ladder

Some kataphatic prayer techniques, however, are not so consistently satisfying. We outgrow them like we outgrow our clothes. That certainly was my experience as a fourteen-year-old after six months of daily meditating and praying over spiritual reading passages. Why does that happen?

Sooner or later, as in any other relationship, we tire of talking and run out of things to say. We want to spend more time listening. The ladder of kataphatic prayer becomes rickety and verges on collapsing. The candle, the music, the Rosary, or the written passage no longer helps us to raise the mind and heart to God. They become a distraction. A hindrance. An obstruction and obstacle. The spiritual consolations dissipate. Language becomes a burden and can no longer convey the thoughts and emotions we are thinking or feeling. We feel a strange attraction to silence but fret and wonder if that is authentic prayer. Like me at fourteen years of age, we begin to think that progress has stopped, God is offended, or something is seriously wrong.

At this point, the person might be tempted to cling tightly to the old method of kataphatic prayer and change, tweak, or adapt it in such a way as to get the spiritual consolations of peace and joy to return. The person changes the music, uses different incense, or turns to another book of the Bible. But all this proves futile. One is stuck and frustrated by a generalized dryness and aridity in prayer.

"The challenge now," Fr. Murray said to me, "is to keep the three Fs."

"The three Fs?" I asked.

"Fidelity, fidelity, fidelity. Don't give up or become discouraged. The dryness is a sign that something is cooking. You're about to turn a corner. Follow the silence and sit in it. When you get distracted, use a prayer word or short phrase to call your attention back to God. And when you get distracted again, as you inevitably will, repeat the word slowly. Return to focusing your attention on God. You'll get distracted. And then you again repeat your prayer word. Follow this method slowly and deliberately."

I returned to Fr. Murray about six weeks later. My spiritual frustration had dissipated. I was getting used to a new form of prayer.

I still remember Fr. Murray's encouragement. "Think of it as your friendship with God blossoming into affection and love. Everything changes. Loving glances, simple touches, and ecstatic silence become the new means of communication."

Though one might not recognize it immediately, the collapse of kataphatic prayer is a sign that God is calling the person to surrender control of their prayer, open the door of the heart even wider, and allow the Spirit to abide within. Perhaps Paul was hinting at this moment when he wrote to the church of Rome, "Likewise the Spirit helps us in our weakness; for we do not know how to pray as we ought, but that very Spirit intercedes with sighs too deep for words" (Romans 8:26). Those deep-seated sighs—sometimes verbalized or visualized—become the content of one's wordless prayer. As one progresses in this new form of prayer, God's grace begins to take over as God puts a foot in the doorway and the Spirit begins to pray within.

This is the landscape of *apophatic* prayer. Apophatic prayer doesn't lean heavily on the five senses, objects, or creation as a ladder to raise the mind and heart to God. It uses silence, simple glances, or just a word or short phrase as the means to open the door of the heart. Even the experience of mindful breathing can be a reminder of the divine presence that surrounds us like the air. With apophatic prayer, less is more. Think of a spouse married for thirty years whose quick glance across the room says it all.

The Jesus Prayer

The Jesus Prayer is a helpful method to practice at the beginning of apophatic prayer. It consists of the simple formula "Lord Jesus Christ, Son of the

Living God, have mercy on me, a sinner." Over time, some people like to customize the prayer by shortening it: "Jesus, have mercy on me, a sinner." "Jesus, mercy." "*Kyrie eleison*." Each person is encouraged to find the right combination of words that work best. Just as mentioning a beloved's name brings to mind wonderful memories and leads to an interior place of silent love and joy, so too praying the name of Jesus sometimes can be a source of spiritual consolation.

Some people like to coordinate the prayer with the breath. They inhale "Lord, Jesus Christ." They hold the breath and pause with "Son of the Living God." They exhale "Have mercy on me, a sinner." I typically start my practice by coordinating the prayer with my breath to settle and center myself. However, I do not hold on to it rigidly as my prayer time continues. Undue concern for breath coordination or overemphasizing it can become a hindrance and distraction.

It's important to remember that this prayer is not a relaxation technique or mantra. Though consoling feelings sometimes descend upon us, this is not the goal of the Jesus Prayer. The goal is an encounter with Jesus by addressing him by name. Like someone whispering the name of their beloved, it is an intensely personal and intimate moment. The very words of the prayer become a reminder that we are in the presence of the Lord and help us to open the heart's door as we become present to the divine presence.

At times, as we slowly recite the Jesus Prayer, we will be attracted to silence. "Follow the silence, Albert," Fr. Murray advised me. "That's where the action is. And when your silence becomes interrupted with distracting thoughts, return to the Jesus Prayer as a reminder in whose presence you sit until you are moved to silence again. Pray it slowly, gently, and deliberately."

Centering Prayer

Over the years, I have discovered two other prayer techniques that help with the natural transition from the words of kataphatic prayer to the silent, loving gaze of apophatic prayer.

The first is promoted by Contemplative Outreach (www.contemplati veoutreach.org) and the late Trappist monk Thomas Keating, OCSO. The method consists of four simple steps:

1. Choose a sacred word as the symbol of your *intention to consent* to God's interior presence and action. Ideally, it should have no spiritual content or emotional significance since that would lead to pondering the word or enjoying the emotions that it signi-fies. The word is simply an arrow that points you or directs your attention to the divine presence and God's action. Think of it as a shepherd's staff that keeps you in line and prevents you from stray-ing away. I find the word "presence" most helpful in this regard. A spiritual directee of mine prefers the word "air," which has no visual or physical content.

2. Sitting comfortably and with eyes closed, settle briefly and silently introduce the sacred word as the symbol of your consent to God's presence and action within.

3. When you catch yourself engaged with or distracted by your thoughts (which include body sensations, feelings, images, and reflections), ever so gently say the sacred word to return to the divine presence and action.

4. At the end of the prayer period, remain in silence with eyes closed for a couple of minutes.

The role of the sacred word is to help our loving gaze focus and stay alert to the presence and action of God. It is not used as a mantra that we slowly and deliberately repeat. It is only introduced when the inevitable distraction arises. It prods and nudges our interior attention back to God.

Christian Meditation

The second technique that is helpful during the transition from kataphatic to apophatic prayer, similar to the Jesus Prayer, is promoted by the World Community of Christian Meditation (https://wccm.org/) and the Benedictine monks Laurence Freeman, OSB, and the late John Main, OSB. This method consists of five steps:

1. Sit down. Sit still and upright. Close your eyes lightly. Sit relaxed but alert. Breathe calmly and regularly.

2. Silently, interiorly begin to say a single word. They recommend the prayer phrase MA-RA-NA-THA (the Aramaic expression, probably used in the early Christian liturgy, meaning "Our Lord, come!" or "Our Lord has come!"—see 1 Corinthians 16:22 and Revelation 22:20). Recite it as four syllables of equal length. Listen to it as you say it, gently but continuously.

3. Do not think or imagine anything—spiritual or otherwise.

4. Thoughts and images are distractions at the time of meditation. Keep returning to the simple repetition of the word.

5. Meditate each morning and evening for twenty to thirty minutes.

Unlike centering prayer where the sacred word is only introduced when one is distracted and needs a nudge to return the loving gaze to God, the prayer phrase in meditation is used with slow and gentle repetition. Like the repetition of the "Hail Mary" when praying the Rosary, its role is to help us stay alert as we focus our gaze, attention, and energies on the divine presence.

Two Important Reminders

In the early days of my apophatic prayer practice, I often caught myself analyzing or evaluating my prayer experiences. I would say to myself, "This is great!" or "I'm making progress!" or "I must remember how I got here so I can return to this same interior place tomorrow." Thankfully, Fr. Murray taught me that these are distractions, revealing I had shifted my attention away from God and onto myself. I needed to catch myself and strengthen my resolve, when these self-reflective distractions intruded, to keep returning to the pure, loving gaze of God facilitated by the nudge of the sacred word or the repetition of the prayer phrase.

"I'm so discouraged! I keep getting distracted when I'm trying to meditate or practice centering prayer." Rosemarie is not alone in her complaint. I often hear it in spiritual direction. I explain to my spiritual directees that the practice in centering prayer is returning to my pure, loving gaze of God when I catch myself being distracted. In Christian meditation, when distracted, I deliberately return to the simple repetition of the prayer phrase. So if I am distracted one hundred times and one hundred times I have said my sacred word to nudge my attention back to God or returned to my intentional repetition of the prayer phrase, then I have correctly practiced centering prayer or Christian meditation one hundred times. That *is* the practice.

Two further points are important to make about distractions. First, distractions are not sins that need to be confessed. On the contrary, they can be great teachers in the spiritual life, often indicating what's important to us, what needs to be done immediately, or what persons or situations need prayer. Simply acknowledging them or even writing them down so we don't forget them can be an effective means of letting them go and returning to our centering prayer or Christian meditation.

Second, actively trying to get rid of distractions becomes another distraction. The goal of centering prayer or Christian meditation is not a Zen-like, thoughtless state of consciousness. Rather, the goal of all prayer is a prayerful surrender not only of the heart whose door is wide open to God but also of the will that is eagerly prepared to respond to any divine invitation or request.

Eucharistic Adoration

Norton is an evangelical Christian who has been committed to the spiritual journey for four years. A few months ago, he read about St. John Vianney's encounter with a farmer who visited his church daily in the small town of Ars, France. The future saint observed the farmer who simply sat in the back pew with no prayer book or rosary. Curious, Vianney asked the farmer how he prayed. The farmer replied, "I look at him and he looks back at me."

The story piqued Norton's curiosity. Norton had heard about the Catholic practice of Eucharistic adoration and had some questions for me. During a spiritual direction session, I answered his questions as best as I could. I sensed he might be interested in trying it out.

"Fifteen minutes from here," I said to him, "is Christ the King Catholic Church. That parish has twenty-four-hour Eucharistic adoration in the side chapel on the east side of the building." Little did I know that information would begin a weekly spiritual practice for Norton.

On Wednesday evenings, he drives to the church. Entering the chapel and knowing this is the Real Presence of Christ in the Eucharist, he kneels in the back pew. He begins his hour with prayers of thanksgiving for the events of the past week. He also mentions those people for whom he has promised to pray.

Unaccustomed to kneeling for a long time and remembering what the farmer did, Norton sits in the pew. He settles into a comfortable position and closes his eyes. He says to himself, "I am in the presence of Christ," and he focuses his interior attention on that presence.

"It's like sitting next to my wife, and I'm not looking at her directly," he told me and continued, "But I am very much aware of her presence beside me. With Christ, I am aware he stands before me."

As soon as his mind wanders—and it does so almost immediately—he opens his eyes and glances at the Blessed Sacrament to reinforce his awareness of the Real Presence. He closes his eyes again and repeats to himself, "I am in the presence of Christ." Within seconds, his mind wanders, he opens his eyes, glances at the Blessed Sacrament, closes his eyes, and reminds himself of the presence of Christ again. He continues this practice for twenty to thirty minutes.

He then picks up his Bible and reads the next story from where he left off in the Gospel of John. He reads the story two or three times. He then puts his Bible aside and ponders the story for its implications in his life. This might take five or ten minutes. He then looks at the Blessed Sacrament and asks, "What do you want me to take away from this passage?" He closes his eyes and waits for a response. Sometimes that reply comes in a word or suggestion: "Love your neighbor." "Forgive Phil." "Respond to that man on the street." Sometimes the reply is a feeling: guilt, peace, thanksgiving, or gratitude.

After about an hour, Norton kneels again and renews his commitment to respond to whatever God, persistently knocking at the door of his heart, asks of him during the upcoming week. He concludes his time with Christ by slowly reciting the Lord's Prayer.

Though not a Roman Catholic, Norton offers one way of opening the door of the heart during Eucharistic adoration when one is in the process of transitioning from kataphatic to apophatic prayer.

Mystical Prayer

For the past five years, Liam has been practicing both the Jesus Prayer and centering prayer. He chooses one for a week or a season and then returns to the other. He is comfortable with the practice of apophatic prayer methods that he sometimes augments with *lectio divina* and spiritual reading.

I was surprised when he recently asked me, "So when will I move into mystical prayer? How do I get there?"

"That's not your decision or choice," I replied. "It's a grace and gift from God."

After that spiritual direction session, I began to reflect on my forty-plus years of doing spiritual direction. In all these years, I can remember only two directees whom I had the privilege of walking with and whom I consider had been given the grace of mystical prayer. Frank was a retired university professor who died at age seventy-four during the Covid pandemic. Fifty-four-year-old Debbie is married, the mother of two adult children, and enjoys writing short stories that occasionally get published.

I once asked Debbie to describe her prayer.

"I become aware of the present moment in which I find myself. And then I go within. I very slowly open the door of my heart. [She is the one responsible for giving me this helpful metaphor.] 'Come, Holy Spirit,' I pray, 'welcome to your temple.' And then I just sit and wait. Sometimes I am filled with a presence that lovingly enters, envelopes me, and opens the windows of my soul. I forget myself as I feel connected to all creation—the immensity of outer space and the blossoming gardenia bush outside—and experience the sorrows and joys of the world—wars, hunger, the birth of a newborn, a new scientific discovery. Sometimes this experience doesn't happen. Sometimes it lasts for five or fifteen minutes and other times, for sixty to ninety minutes. The length of time never depends on me. When the experience ends, I am left with a deeper hunger and thirst for God that is never satisfied."

Six points are worth noting from the spiritual tradition and Debbie's experience.

First, we should never explicitly seek mystical prayer since that is a form of spiritual selfishness and expresses ingratitude for the gift of prayer that God freely offers anyone who opens the door of the heart. The desire for mystical prayer becomes a distraction and hindrance that places more emphasis on the gift than the Giver. Deceased Frank once put it this way, "I want the Spouse, not the wedding ring."

Second, a person cannot think, will, or pray oneself to mystical prayer. It cannot be attained through human effort nor is it a natural consequence of apophatic prayer since some have experienced it as a result of kataphatic prayer. All a person can do is open the door of the heart through prayer techniques and be receptive to whatever God offers or asks.

Third, mystical prayer is a pure gift and only given to a few. God is responsible for who receives it and when it is given. We will never know why God chooses some people to experience it.

Like a shooting star, it apparently comes out of nowhere. It doesn't always happen with the snap of a finger or the folding of hands. When it does occur, it is sometimes fleeting and sometimes prolonged. God is totally in charge as the Spirit prays within.

Fifth, it is not an other-worldly experience that pulls a person out of our worldly existence to some spiritual la-la land as is sometimes portrayed in art. Just the opposite is true. As Debbie gives witness, it plunges a person more deeply into our material world and gives rise to an extraordinary compassion where, united with creation and humanity, one feels the depths of human despair and the heights of human delight.

Finally, the experience of mystical prayer leaves a person wanting more. In one of the great paradoxes of the spiritual life, it satisfies in a way that is unsatisfying and deepens the hunger and thirst for God.

We begin our relationship with God by opening the door of the heart. That relationship is maintained and nurtured through kataphatic prayer practices that help us to express the feelings, desires, and longings of the heart. Sooner or later, like any other relationship in our lives, we grow weary of words. The words collapse and deflate and can no longer contain what's in the heart. We begin to feel a strange attraction to silence. When that attraction arises, we follow the silence, knowing full well that it is not an empty silence but an intimate silence with God, who has a history with us of love and forgiveness.

Reflection Questions

1. When have I felt the attraction to silence during my prayer time? How did I respond to it then? How would I respond to it now after reading this chapter?

2. What are my thoughts and reaction to prayer techniques such as centering prayer and Christian meditation? What have been my experiences with them?

3. Are there any activities like gardening, cooking, or feeding an infant that bring me into the presence of God? What are they?

7

EXPERIENCING SPIRITUAL DARKNESS, PART 1

Spiritual darkness is a grace that facilitates detachment and purification.

Xavier has been in spiritual direction for more than seven years. He's quite faithful to a monthly session. He is sincere, honest, and very open about what's going on in his life.

"It's been a little over three months since my brother died," he told me. "He was my best friend. We talked on the phone every day and I always sought his advice on just about everything. My wife sometimes complained that I was too dependent on him—but like I said, he was my best friend. Since his death, I've been in a funk. I don't want to get out of bed in the morning. And once I do, I find it hard just to focus on the task at hand. I don't want to be around people, including my wife and children. I've lost interest in just about everything. And in the past couple of weeks, that includes my spiritual life.

"I'm beginning to feel like God has abandoned me. I'm so angry about the way he has thrown me in the trash can like an old magazine. I've been so faithful to him, and he's just thumbed his nose up at me. I'm not interested in daily prayer. I even find going to Mass boring and burdensome, so I've stopped going.

"I feel like everything that I once held near and dear—my brother, my interest in relationships, my spiritual life—has been stripped away. The best way I can explain it is that I feel the pain of my humanity with nothing to lean on or distract me or give me hope."

Was Xavier depressed or was something else going on?

Depression

Initially, Xavier's emotional reaction to his brother's death betrayed the earmarks of depression. At its basic level, depression is the emotional state of feeling sad. It has a continuum from feeling "blue" that we all experience on occasion to mild melancholy to debilitating hopelessness. Depression's signs, often manifested physically and emotionally, include the following:

- feelings of sadness, emptiness, worthlessness, and guilt;
- angry outbursts and irritability;
- loss of interest in sex, hobbies, and sports;
- change in sleep patterns, appetite, and weight;
- lack of energy and reduced concentration on simple tasks;
- restlessness and anxiety;
- unexplained physical problems like a backache or queasy stomach;
- suicidal ideations.

A depressed person does not have to exhibit all these signs. Even one, experienced to a mild or debilitating degree, can be a sign of a depressed state and can influence one's lifestyle, work, and family relationships. Xavier exhibited at least three signs: loss of libido, change in his sleep pattern, and lack of energy and concentration.

Though depression can be genetic or hormonal and might need clinical observation and medication, in most cases it is the direct emotional reaction to an unexpected or continuing negative life event. In Xavier's case, it was the death of his brother.

How do we respond to depression? Sometimes a simple form of relaxation, exercise, cooking a meal, or reading a book can pull us out of the doldrums of feeling "blue." For mild depression to debilitating hopelessness, the strategy is somewhat different. Because attempts at self-diagnosis and self-medication often prolong the emotional pain, it's best to seek out a competent clinical professional. Professional help is sometimes best augmented with:

- getting regular rest, exercise, eating healthily, learning how to manage stress, changing negative thought patterns;
- learning how to express emotions appropriately;
- connecting with friends, relatives, and support groups;
- and sometimes medication.

A combination of these factors can help us cope with mild depression to debilitating hopelessness.

Spiritual Darkness

At times, as happened in Xavier's reaction to his brother's death, depression and hopelessness can affect our spiritual lives by morphing into an experience of spiritual darkness. Spiritual darkness is the collapse and breakdown of the spiritual life as we know it. In its beginning stage, it forces us to come face-to-face with the inability to make ourselves happy and whole. As it deepens, we fumble and tumble as we struggle to feel our way through the darkness. Our prayer techniques prove futile and fruitless. The lights and neon signs that illumined our journey and offered us consolation and direction go out. We question our past motives and actions and become hypersensitive to our human weakness and fragility. We are riddled with confusion as the God we once knew is painfully silent—or seemingly obliterated. At its foundation, spiritual darkness forces us to confront our idolatry with the sobering question "Who really is in charge of my life?"

As a spiritual director and pilgrim on the spiritual journey, I have observed and experienced the broad spectrum or continuum of spiritual darkness. Those who are faithful to daily prayer inevitably experience the early segments of the spectrum while some of the more mature and seasoned pilgrims will be plunged into the later segments. The continuum of spiritual darkness begins by exposing human fragility and then moves to purifying the deep recesses of the heart. I'll discuss the beginning spectrum of spiritual darkness in this chapter and the deeper purification in the next chapter.

Childhood and Early Upbringing

Xavier's experience of feeling stripped was most telling. "The best way I can explain it, is that I feel the pain of my humanity with nothing to lean on or distract me or give me hope." The loss of his brother—"my best friend"—unearthed something he consciously had never known. He depended upon his brother too much and had put too many expectations on their relationship. That awareness points directly to the purpose of the beginning segment of spiritual darkness. It exposes our human fragility.

Childhood and early adolescence are critical—perhaps the most critical—times in a person's development. There are certain tasks that need to be addressed and completed if we are to become healthy adults. These developmental tasks include the following:

- the feeling of being loved unconditionally with the physical and emotional security that it provides;
- schooling in socially acceptable behavior and sharing skills to respond appropriately as a boy or girl to playmates, siblings, parents, relatives, and adults;
- the development of conscience, morality, and values;
- the development of healthy dependence and later independence.

These developmental tasks will form the foundation on which a person will build one's life as an adult.

Unfortunately, most of us do not complete all the important developmental tasks of childhood in a healthy way. Often, without malicious intent, our parents, siblings, and friends hinder us from completing the tasks. Katie, for example, knows her obsession with being acknowledged and accepted by others is a result of always feeling overshadowed by her two brothers, who she feels received more parental attention than she. Sometimes parents and friends pass on their own unhealthy and incomplete response to a particular task. Jim was raised by parents who taught him distrust and dislike for certain minorities. Sally grew up thinking that her self-image and self-worth depended on her performance in the classroom, and now, as an adult, she is driven to be an overachiever. Sometimes the completion of the developmental tasks can be sabotaged by a traumatic event.

Of my parent's five children, I was closest to my father. My father and I shared a close bond that baffled my mother and siblings. As a thirteen-year-old, I felt betrayed, heartbroken, and devastated when my father chose to die by suicide. Thirty years after his death, a retired Franciscan friar whom I deeply respected challenged me with the question "Why is it, Albert, you always seem to be looking for a father figure?" It didn't take me long to discover the origin of my search. No one gets out of childhood and early adolescence unscathed.

We enter adulthood, either consciously like Katie or unconsciously like me, aware that something is missing in our lives. What we lacked or *think* we lacked in childhood and early adolescence—perception forms our reality—opens an emotional void. I like to think of it as a hole in the heart. That hole is the result of a harsh word we remember ("You're stupid!"), a lesson we were taught ("Money and fame are the measures of success!"), or a traumatic event we endured (e.g., the death of a family member, the divorce of one's parents, the destruction caused by a natural disaster). As adults, we go on a restless, quixotic search to fill the void, to plug up the hole in the heart. Why? Because we mistakenly believe that our happiness and wholeness depend on grabbing what was missing in our upbringing.

The Empty Ps

And so begins our habit of opening the door of the heart and stuffing it with trifles and trinkets—a visible sign that we are not satisfied. Stuffed hearts are like the bloated stomachs of starving children: they betray our hunger, not our satisfaction.

The trifles and trinkets we seek are typically one or more of the empty Ps: power, prestige, position, people, possessions, productivity, popularity, pleasure, and praise. We constantly are looking outside ourselves, thinking one or more of these empty Ps can fill the hole in the heart and satisfy our deep-seated restlessness. In effect, one or more of the empty Ps become an idol we worship.

Clarence believes that *power, prestige*, and *position* will slack his thirst to be recognized and boost his self-image. His coworkers call him a "power grabber" behind his back. Without these three Ps, he fears cowering under his childhood bed each day like a punished puppy. With them, he feels puffed up, important, and doesn't hesitate to bark his way through the week with endless demands.

Angie, adopted by an older couple whom she felt never really loved her, once confessed to me, "I'm looking for the perfect husband but up until now, every person I've dated has disappointed me." Like some people, she has bought into the lie that *people* can make her happy. Her heart is filled with memories of former boyfriends who have not lived up to her unspoken expectation that "your mission is to make me feel loved." Each relationship ended with Angie being frustrated with herself and angry at the other.

In our consumer society, who hasn't been deceived into thinking *possessions* can make us happy? Those raised in lower-income families particularly are prone to buy into the lie that having the latest cell phone, the big house, the expensive automobile, or fashionable clothes will lead to a life of fulfillment. Once they acquire the latest gadget or indulge in the latest fad, the momentary and fleeting satisfaction of having or experiencing it quickly dissipates. And off they go again in search of another toy.

Joey is a workaholic who throws himself into *productivity*. Remembering being called "lazy" by his parents, he defines himself by the fruit of his labors and so keeps cranking out the work so that others will admire, need, and, most of all, notice him. His fear of sickness and mandatory retirement is indicative that his self-worth and self-esteem are tied up in what he does. Without work, he would feel useless and worthless—and "lazy."

Like a Hollywood star arriving for the Oscars, Ruth knows how to posture and pose to show her best side. She is obsessed with *popularity*. Her friends are very much aware that behind her performance are the painful questions of an insecure childhood: "Do you like me? Am I okay? Do you find me acceptable?" The self-acceptance that Ruth never learned for herself, she begs from others.

In a society that prides itself on having a medication for every headache or heartache, it's easy to chase after *pleasure*. Those raised in families where an addiction was prevalent are especially prone to search for forms of diversion and entertainment. The internet has made this a virtual journey, since we no longer need to get into a car and head to the adult bookstore, the shopping mall, or the airport to catch a flight to Las Vegas. Harmless and exciting as these distractions apparently seem, they can easily develop into unhealthy compulsions that ultimately lead to full-blown addictions to alcohol, sex, drugs, romance, gambling, shopping, or food.

Never feeling affirmed, appreciated, and approved growing up, Robert spends his days in search of *praise*. He is always fishing for a compliment about his artistic talent and angling for a pat on the back. When neither comes, he goes into a funk and begins a well-rehearsed, self-critical inner monologue.

Let me note two important points about the empty Ps.

First, there is nothing inherently wrong with having one or more of them. As a matter of fact, the Ps help us become healthy, assured, and mature individuals. They become a hindrance, however, when we equate our happiness with possessing them. If we become so obsessed with one or more of them, we allow them to distract and divert our attention away from opening the door of the heart to God and responding to divine invitations and requests.

Jane recently reminded me of a second point. "The empty Ps mean nothing to me. I'm not obsessed with any of them," she proudly announced. It's important to remember that the enumeration of the empty Ps is meant to be more evocative than descriptive. I have yet to meet a person who is totally free from the ego's obsession with self-concern (prestige, popularity, praise), self-interest (power, productivity), self-gratification (people, pleasure), or self-preservation (possessions).

Your childhood deficiency shapes the contours of the idol you place in your heart and obsessively seek to appease and worship. One way of naming that idol is to ask yourself, "What do I need *in order to be happy?*" The answer to that question becomes the litany you pray before the altar in your heart.

EXPERIENCING SPIRITUAL DARKNESS, PART 1

Detachment

Many people spend the first half of their lives running after the empty Ps to enshrine them on their heart's altar. But then at midlife, some people discover the futility of any or all the Ps to make them feel happy and whole. The New Testament expresses this heart-wrenching wisdom with the challenge of detachment. Seven quotes are worth mentioning:

- "Do not think that I have come to bring peace to the earth; I have not come to bring peace but a sword. For I have come to set a man against his father, and a daughter against her mother, and a daughter-in-law against her mother-in-law, and one's foes will be members of one's own household. Whoever loves father or mother more than me is not worthy of me; and whoever loves son or daughter more than me is not worthy of me; and whoever does not take up the cross and follow me is not worthy of me. Those who find their life will lose it, and those who lose their life for my sake will find it." (Matthew 10:34-39; see also Luke 9:23, 14:26)

- "He must increase, but I must decrease." (John 3:30)

- But if we have died with Christ, we believe that we will also live with him. (Romans 6:8)

- For freedom Christ has set us free. Stand firm, therefore, and do not submit again to a yoke of slavery. (Galatians 5:1)

- And it is no longer I who live, but it is Christ who lives in me. And the life I now live in the flesh I live by faith in the Son of God, who loved me and gave himself for me. (Galatians 2:20)

- More than that, I regard everything as loss because of the surpassing value of knowing Christ Jesus my Lord. For his sake I have

"

THE FIRST SEGMENT OF SPIRITUAL DARKNESS' SPECTRUM IS THAT IT DESCENDS, THREATENS, AND OFTEN REMOVES THE EMPTY Ps WE THINK WE NEED IN ORDER TO BE HAPPY. IT FORCES US TO FACE THE HOLE IN THE HEART.

"

suffered the loss of all things, and I regard them as rubbish, in order that I may gain Christ. (Philippians 3:8)

• Put to death, therefore, whatever in you is earthly: fornication, impurity, passion, evil desire, and greed (which is idolatry). (Colossians 3:5)

These passages remind us that our desperate search for something outside ourselves to fill the hole in the heart—be it a physical possession, an emotional need, or a treasured relationship—is futile and, more importantly, becomes a roadblock on the spiritual journey.

And yet, we tenaciously cling to the empty Ps as if we could not live without them. This is witnessed in Jesus' encounter with the rich young man (see Matthew 19:16-30; Mark 10:17-31; Luke 18:18-30). By his own admission, the rich young man was faithful to the commandments of God. But he clearly hungered for more. Hearing Jesus' advice that he sell all his possessions, give the money to the poor, and then follow Jesus, the man went away sad. Mark adds the detail that the man was initially "shocked" (10:22). His grief was caused by the emotional hold his many possessions had on him. Possessed by his own possessions, the rich young man hesitated to satisfy the deeper hunger of his heart. We are not told if he later followed Jesus' advice.

Like the rich young man, most of us refuse to freely embrace the New Testament challenge of detachment and the call to freedom. This is precisely the grace—I use the word deliberately—of the first segment of spiritual darkness' spectrum: it descends, threatens, and often removes the empty Ps we think we need in order to be happy. It forces us to face the hole in the heart "with nothing to lean on or distract me or give me hope," to quote Xavier. It is the experience of our human fragility. Painful, jarring, and confusing as it is, this segment proclaims the startling truth that fifth-century Augustine of Hippo wrote at the beginning of his *Confessions*: "You have made us for yourself, O Lord, and our hearts are restless until they rest in you."

The Prayer of Job

How does one pray in the early days of spiritual darkness? How do we respond to the destruction of the idol we consider so valuable and in which we invested so much time and energy?

We get an important cue from the story of Job. At the beginning of the story, Job is stripped of seemingly everything: his family, his worldly goods, and his own physical health. Yet amid his misery, while he sits atop a dunghill, he cries out: "Naked I came from my mother's womb, and naked shall I return there; the LORD gave, and the LORD has taken away; blessed be the name of the LORD" (Job 1:21).

I would never recommend this prayer immediately after the loss of a home to a tornado, the death of a spouse, or the loss of a job. It's important that a person first grieve what has been lost. And each one does that in one's own time and in one's own way.

Moreover, we should never put a spiritual Band-Aid or throw holy water on someone's pain at the loss of any empty P by saying, "This is God's will" or "This will bring you closer to God" or "This will turn into a blessing in disguise" or "This will make you stronger." Such words are cold, cruel, and unsympathetic.

It's sometimes helpful to give voice to the pain of grief with its anger and frustration toward God by praying the psalms of lament. Psalms such as 13, 22, 42, 60, 71, 86, and 142 can be helpful in this regard.

Paula lost her beloved husband of thirty years, Tom, more than three years ago. Only recently has the grief begun to dissipate. She now can pray the prayer of Job that acknowledges the gift, grace, and blessing Tom was to her. With Job, she can explicitly affirm that there is only one true God, a divine almsgiver who lavishly provides us everything—and is not immune from taking gifts away.

The Timing of Darkness

Midlife is prime time for the first segment of darkness to descend, to make us aware of how we have turned one or more of the empty Ps into an idol, and to call us to detachment and freedom. A gracious surrender to this darkness is the beginning of spiritual wisdom.

However, the first segment of darkness is not confined to midlife. It can descend at any time. I've had directees who have experienced it in their mid-twenties and early thirties. No matter its timing, spiritual darkness always poses a shock as it did to the Marcan rich young man (see Mark 10:22). That shock is sometimes assuaged through unhealthy behaviors that can easily become addictive. Freddie turned to alcohol after he was demoted, while Diane turned to compulsive shopping when her reputation was publicly destroyed. Both behaviors were attempts to numb the shock of confronting human fragility.

But that shock can also be the catalyst for developing a reflective lifestyle and getting serious about the spiritual journey. Three years after reaching the pinnacle of his dream career, forty-one-year-old Doug woke up one morning, looked himself in the mirror, and asked, "Is this all there is to life? Surely there must be more." That realization led him to begin spiritual direction. Diagnosed with cancer in her mid-twenties, Darlene made a moral inventory of her life, went to confession, and began volunteering at a soup kitchen. It dawns on me as I write this that without being consciously aware that I was responding to the shock of my father's suicide, I made the commitment to daily prayer the year after his death. Some people experience the early spectrum of spiritual darkness as a continual grief that blankets their vision; others experience it, usually in hindsight, as the *other* side of grace.

Spiritual darkness frees us from the illusion that we can cure our heart's restlessness with the empty Ps. For many, it sets them on a deeper journey in search of the "God of all consolation" (2 Corinthians 1:3) who alone can heal the hole in the heart. That interior journey sets the stage for the possible continuation of spiritual darkness that purifies the deepest recesses of the heart.

REFLECTION QUESTIONS

1. When have I experienced a traumatic event that left me depressed? Did my depression have any effect on my spiritual life? Why or why not?

2. To be happy, what do I need?

3. After grieving a disappointment, loss, or tragedy, have I been able to pray the prayer of Job? Why or why not?

8

EXPERIENCING SPIRITUAL DARKNESS, PART 2

Spiritual darkness is a grace that facilitates detachment
and purification.

Byron has an uncanny ability to distinguish a sunrise from a sunset. When I've tested him with photographs on my cell phone, he's correct nine out of ten times. I once asked him how he could tell the difference.

"Sunrises have a natural glow to themselves that pull me out of myself. Just as the sun rises over the horizon, I feel this strange pull to look up and beyond myself. Sunsets are different. They are more striking, beautiful, and colorful. As I behold their splendor, I feel moved to go within, to become reflective. I know sunrises and sunsets might look the same to you. But for me, there's a clear difference, and they affect me differently."

As I reflected on what Byron had said, it dawned on me that his distinction provides a metaphor for the spectrum of spiritual darkness. Many people begin the journey of life at sunrise. They are looking beyond themselves, specifically for one or more of the empty Ps to satisfy the restlessness of the heart. It's only in the evening that the spiritual journey truly begins.

From Twilight to Dusk

As one opens the door of the heart, God enters, empties the heart of its idols, and prepares it to become a new sanctuary of the divine. The inability of the empty Ps to fill the void of a childhood deficiency and the awareness that only God can satisfy the restlessness of the human heart are illuminating insights. I liken them to Byron's description of an evening sunset.

As I mentioned at the conclusion of the previous chapter, the twilight of this sunset motivates many to become reflective, look within, and begin the life of prayer. These people begin searching for prayer techniques that help them establish a "divine dialogue," as Jamie once called it. They use the words of kataphatic prayer as mentioned in chapter 6. They might pray the Rosary. They might meditate on the words of Scripture. They might spend time praying from the neck down and telling God about the day's events and their reactions. They are filled with pride as they think they are making progress on the spiritual journey.

And then, after six months or so, their prayer naturally dries up. The person finds meditation on Scripture tedious and unsatisfying and is unable to stir up any thoughts. This gives rise to the fear that one is regressing spiritually. And, as I mentioned in chapter 6, the attraction to silence begins.

The gradual movement from kataphatic to apophatic prayer, where words cannot convey what only silence can, is likened to dusk. It can be a bit disconcerting at first as one questions whether this is authentic prayer. But if one remains faithful, the eyes gradually adjust to a darkened prayer that paradoxically nurtures and nourishes the relationship with God. One experiences this not only as a lifting of the spiritual darkness but also as a reprieve.

Toward Midnight

The vast majority of faithful pilgrims journey to this point and remain there for the rest of their lives. They are content to leave the door of their hearts ajar and respond to the God of surprise and disguise who knocks at the door and, like the persistent widow in Jesus' parable (see Luke 18:1-5), entices and cajoles a response for the sake of the kingdom of peace, love, and justice. Occasionally the Spirit enters and prays within these people. They relish the allure of silence that speaks of a love beyond all telling.

For a chosen few, however, there is more to come. Spiritual darkness is progressive; if it returns, it often picks up where it left off. Sometimes its function is only to let people again experience their human fragility and the inability of the empty Ps to satisfy the heart's restlessness. Other times its function is to deepen the silence. Occasionally its function is more challenging.

Seventy-year-old Charlie, a widower for seven years, had been on the spiritual journey for fifty years and experienced the more challenging function of spiritual darkness. I suspected he had been chosen by God, for reasons unknown, to move into midnight. He mentioned two things that caught my attention.

"I'm struggling with sexual desires," he told me. "Memories and images from my past are constantly intruding into my prayer. I find myself focusing on fantasies that I haven't thought about in decades. And it's not that I'm actively digging them up or thinking about them. They seem to be coming from outside myself. The devil can really be tricky, huh?"

It seemed to me these desires were not temptations from the devil. Rather, something else was going on. Sexual memories are sometimes the medication we take to avoid feeling the hole in the heart and our human fragility. We lean on them for distraction and comfort. The spiritual tradition firmly attests to the fact that as spiritual darkness returns and descends,

"

DURING THE DEEPER SEGMENTS OF SPIRITUAL DARKNESS, WE CAN'T ALWAYS SEE WHAT GOD SPECIFICALLY IS ASKING OF US. . . . THIS GIVES RISE TO A RESENTMENT AND CONFUSION THAT EMBODY A DEEP RESISTANCE TO CONTINUING THE JOURNEY FOR FEAR WE MIGHT LOSE OURSELVES.

"

it reaches into the depths of the psyche and transforms repressed memories and desires. At this moment in his life, Charlie was being asked to deliberately detach himself from the medication of sexual thoughts and hand it over to the Divine Physician. This was not a temptation but a purification.

Two months later, Charlie's mood confirmed for me that he was in the throes of midnight.

"I'm ticked off and have had it with God. All my life, since my twenties, I've tried my best to be faithful to God. I've given him everything I've got. And he doesn't seem to be content with that. He wants more, and I don't have any more to give. I resent the fact that he's treating me this way."

I affirmed Charlie's fidelity and yes to God. "But, Charlie, you have to understand," I continued, "God is now asking you to say yes again, but on a deeper level. Don't resist it. Just try to lean into it—to open the door of your heart even wider to the mystery of God's grace in your life."

During the deeper segments of spiritual darkness, we can't always see what God specifically is asking of us. We might intuit it but aren't certain. Like Charlie, we just know that something more is being requested. We can't say no to God but we struggle to say yes because we are uncertain of what is being asked. It's as if this "jealous God" (Exodus 34:14) is asking us to write a blank check. This gives rise to a resentment and confusion that embody a deep resistance to continuing the journey for fear we might lose ourselves. And lose ourselves we will, as we decrease and he increases (see John 3:30).

Midnight

God plunges a few pilgrims into the darkness of midnight with its final purification of the heart and one's image of God.

People are in the throes of midnight when they are beset with a spirit of dizziness, confusion, and perplexity. As spiritual darkness purifies the deepest recesses of their hearts, these people become hypersensitive and highly attuned to what is and is not of God. Think of it as the conscience at a heightened level of attentiveness, on overload. Though it might mask as scrupulosity, it is not. Rather, it is a new sensitivity of love. These people are thrown into confusion as they question whether they are really following the will of God, which is their one living desire. Plagued by doubts, they can find no inner peace.

This is indicative of a deep purification. Formerly there were elements of spiritual pride lurking in the heart as the person felt certain, secure, and "right with God," as one spiritual directee told me. Now one is being purified of the pride that comes with being chosen by grace. The person is challenged to let go of all control and walk with blind faith. The words of the risen Christ to Peter speak to this:

> "Very truly, I tell you, when you were younger, you used
> to fasten your own belt and to go wherever you wished.
> But when you grow old, you will stretch out your hands,
> and someone else will fasten a belt around you and
> take you where you do not wish to go. . . . Follow me."
> (John 21:18, 19)

The ego is being purged and cleansed as the person does what "might" be the will of God, even while patiently enduring the cross of self-doubt.

And it's not only the conscience and ego that are purged and cleansed; it's also our image of God. We easily mistake our *image* of God *for* God. But it is not; it's simply a picture. A treasured portrait. A precious photograph. An image that has gotten us through difficult, trying, and even traumatic times. Suddenly that picture is torn up and thrown aside by the likes of whom we do not know.

One is left feeling God-less. For some people, it feels as if God has disappeared. Having prayed to and served this God all their lives, these people now feel abandoned, orphaned, and without any wheel, map, or lighthouse to guide them through the night. The seas become rough and the ship of the spiritual life—one's relationship with God—takes on water and violently bounces.

This is analogous to the experience of Jesus on Calvary. His image of God, pronounced in his native Aramaic as *Abba*, was shattered as he hung on the cross. Instead of addressing his Father with this usual term of intimacy, he chose to pray Psalm 22:2 with the more distant name for God: "My God, my God, [in Aramaic, *Eloi, Eloi*] why have you forsaken me?" (Mark 15:34; see Matthew 27:46)

Two points are worthy of note.

We can have our image of God threatened, even destroyed, without being in the depths of midnight per se. Tragic and traumatic events can cause us to question our treasured picture of God. "Why is God allowing this to happen?" is a sure indication that our thoughts about the mystery of God are inadequate, secondhand, and need to be purified. St. Augustine offered sage advice when he wrote, "If you understand it, it's not God."[3]

Second, it's important to remember that feelings are an unsure guide in the spiritual life and cannot be trusted. Even if we feel abandoned and orphaned by God, we are always in the presence of God, who is like the air we breathe. "In him we live and move and have our being" (Acts 17:28), as Paul preached at the Areopagus. Sometimes our emotional reaction to tragedy blinds us to the intuition, knowledge, or experience of God's presence.

The destruction of our image of God has consequences for our faith, hope, and love. Our faith is purged and cleansed as we move to an expression of faith that is less about rational assent and more about blind trust as a way of living: "For we walk by faith, not by sight" (2 Corinthians 5:7). Hope is transformed from an amorphous expectation to a blessed conviction "that all things work together for good for those who love God, who are called according to his purpose" (Romans 8:28). Love becomes a selfless desire "to lay down one's life for one's friends" (John 15:13).

Though only a few people experience the full and prolonged spiritual darkness of midnight, many people experience hints of midnight's darkness in depressing or traumatic experiences that confound, confuse, and disrupt the spiritual journey: the death of a loved one, the loss incurred by a natural disaster, a financial disaster, the public exposure of one's darkest secrets, the diagnosis of a life-threatening disease. After the initial shock with its accompanying anger and confusion, one's ultimate response to a painful experience determines whether it will become an obstacle or an opportunity for spiritual growth.

The Coming of Dawn

The few who do experience the darkness of midnight occasionally find themselves inching toward dawn as they catch glimmers of light. And with that morning light, as Byron suggests, one's attention is moved beyond oneself—but this time, not toward any of the empty Ps, but to the needs and necessities of the world.

Though feeling capable of committing every possible sin, the few people who are called from midnight to the dawn have been purified of all spiritual pride as well as egotistical impulses and selfish desires. The Spirit fills the heart, and these chosen few are transformed by grace into people of love, peace, joy, patience, kindness, faithfulness, generosity, gentleness, and self-control (see Galatians 5:22-23). They are propelled forward with a continual burst of ministerial energy for the kingdom and become living incarnations of the kingdom's peace, love, and justice. The door of the heart and the windows of the soul are wide open as these people graciously and unhesitatingly surrender to even the smallest or most strenuous request of our persistent God.

St. Charles de Foucauld's Prayer of Abandonment

Before his sudden death in 2020, seventy-four-year-old Frank was in the throes of midnight. He had been experiencing it for seventeen months. It was a time of intense spiritual purification and transformation. Sitting and listening to him, I was in awe of the mystery of God's grace and constantly reminded of what God said through the prophet Isaiah: "For my thoughts are not your thoughts, nor are your ways my ways, says the LORD" (Isaiah 55:8).

When I asked him how he managed to remain faithful, Frank told me how, for more than nine years, he had been praying the Prayer of Abandonment written by Charles de Foucauld. "I pray it when I wake up and when I go to bed. Over time, it has become the true desire of my heart," he whispered.

Charles de Foucauld, canonized in 2020, wrote the prayer in his thirties before leaving the Trappist Order to become a hermit. He placed it on the lips of Christ in his final moments on the cross. The prayer expresses the primary and fundamental stance of every pilgrim on the spiritual journey: surrender and acceptance. It sings of a person who has thrown open the door of the heart to God and is ready to respond to any divine invitation or request.

> Father, I abandon myself into your hands;
> do with me what you will.
> Whatever you may do, I thank you:
> I am ready for all, I accept all.
>
> Let only your will be done in me,
> and in all your creatures—I wish no more than this,
> O Lord.
>
> Into your hands I commend my soul:
> I offer it to you with all the love of my heart,

for I love you, Lord, and so need to give myself,
to surrender myself into your hands without reserve,
and with boundless confidence,
for you are my Father.

Though we often experience God's grace as light, insight, consolation, and strength, we fail to remember that spiritual darkness is also a grace, the *other* side of grace. It challenges us to confront and detach from the idols in our hearts. It also purifies our hearts, rids us of spiritual pride, and cleanses our flimsy images of God. When God knocks on the door of the heart, we open it, not knowing if we are going to be steeped in light or in darkness. That is the reward—and risk—of surrender and acceptance.

REFLECTION QUESTIONS

1. When did I begin to take the spiritual journey seriously? What, if any, was the precipitating event that challenged me to become reflective and begin the life of prayer?

2. When has my image of God been challenged or destroyed? How do I think about God now?

3. What thoughts or feelings arise as I reflect on the words of St. Charles de Foucauld's Prayer of Abandonment?

9

BECOMING A
CONTEMPLATIVE IN
ACTION

*Fidelity to prayer, while reminding me of my brokenness,
transforms my lifestyle from compulsion to contemplation.*

As I've mentioned time and again in this book, the purpose of prayer is to make us prayerful—that is, aware and attentive to the numerous ways the God of surprise and disguise knocks on the door of the heart. With that knock comes the invitation to help make the kingdom of peace, love, and justice a reality. The awareness of the knock and our response to the invitation gradually transform our lives from one of compulsion to one of contemplation. We become, in the words of an early follower of Ignatius of Loyola, "contemplatives in action."[4] Contemplatives in action are aware of God's knocking, readily open the heart's door, and allow God's grace to transform their thoughts, words, and actions so they can build the kingdom of peace, love, and justice.

What are some characteristics of a contemplative in action? How do prayerfulness and grace change us? Let's explore some of the features and habits of a contemplative lifestyle that have transformed the lives of ordinary people.

Childlike Wonder and Awe

"I've been in the convent for twenty-two years," Sr. Marcia told me. "When I think back to my time before entering and after entering religious life, I notice a huge difference. It was as if, for the first thirty years of my life, I was living in black and white. Don't get me wrong: it was a great life, and I enjoyed my freedom. But I was living on autopilot, doing everything by rote and routine. That gave my life a dull luster because I was blind and deaf to its spiritual dimension.

"During my years of religious formation when I became serious about my prayer life, I began to see everything in living color. I noticed how God puts a blooming rose bush in my garden just for my enjoyment. I experienced God consoling me in the cool breeze of the evening when I took my walk. I felt God nudging me to be a kinder and more charitable person in the ordinary circumstances of my day. It's so surprising: it's as if my entire life has become this beautiful majestic cathedral where I discover something of God in all the nooks and crannies of my day."

As I listened to Sr. Marcia, it was evident to me that she had become a contemplative in action. No longer living on autopilot, she had strong intuitions of God's presence in everything that surrounded her. And her surprise was indicative of a life of wonder, awe, fascination, and amazement. During her years of prayer, she had become more attentive and aware of the God of surprise and disguise.

Living in the Present Moment

There's another indication that Sr. Marcia had become a contemplative in action. Her discovery of God "in all the nooks and crannies of my day" is a telltale sign that she lives in "the sacrament of the present moment," to use the expression of the nineteenth-century spiritual classic *Abandonment to Divine Providence*, traditionally ascribed to the Jesuit Jean-Pierre de Caussade.

Some people, dwelling on the guilt of a past action or the nostalgia of "the good old days," get stuck in the past. Others tumble into the future with worries and anxiety. Fixation on the past or future hinders us from seeing, hearing, and experiencing God's persistent knock on the door of the heart in the present moment. As we walk the journey of prayer, we become more and more attentive to the divine presence in the here and now even after our designated prayer time. This is prayerfulness. Every moment becomes an encounter with the divine, a "sacrament." That sacramental presence is sometimes manifested and discovered in the blooming flower in front of us or in the hungry, the thirsty, the stranger, the naked, the sick, or the prisoner before us (see Matthew 25:31-46).

Gratitude, Generosity, and Gentleness

Adam once said to me, "I used to be a control freak. I was rigid and opinionated and believed my way of doing things was the only way. All my achievements were a result of my hard work. That gave me a sense of entitlement and made me extraordinarily selfish and greedy.

"Over the years, however, I've discovered that everything in my life is a gift. That includes my wife and family, my job, the clothes on my back, and the food on the table. And yes, even my achievements. It's all a result of God's abiding care and concern for me. Gratitude has become the continual attitude of my day as I simply try to respond to whatever God is asking of me right now. That's my mission in life: to do the will of God. Consequently, I see myself becoming generous both with my time and my talents. I'm more flexible and willing to embrace change."

Prayer has made Adam more mindful of the lavish generosity of God. That awareness fuels a sense of gratitude and thanksgiving as he responds to every divine request, knowing full well that he is helping to build God's kingdom of peace, love, and justice. He has gone from having a clenched fist and self-absorbed heart to living with open hands and an altruistic, expansive heart. The door of his heart and the windows of his soul are wide open.

Patience, Sensitivity to Others, and Self-Acceptance

"You used to be so driven," my brother recently reminded me. "You approached each situation like a bull in a china shop. You never showed any respect for the damage or injury you caused." I could have added that I remember at times being paralyzed with worry and anxiety. I also developed the awful habit of comparing myself with others.

Somewhere along the line, those rough edges were smoothed by God's grace. I saw myself becoming less anxious and grew in patience as I learned that life is a process to be lived and loved, not a destination where one arrived. "Enjoy the journey" became my motto in my late fifties. I became sensitive to how my words and actions affected other people. And I learned to accept my weaknesses, foibles, quirks, and idiosyncrasies. I also discovered that everyone has unique gifts and talents that are to be celebrated. My sense of being in competition with others disappeared.

Acceptance of God's Will

I immediately saw how grace had transformed Sr. Carolyn into a contemplative in action. She made a startling discovery in the past year.

"I came to the monastery because I wanted to be a contemplative. I had hopes and dreams of living in the loving presence of God at every moment. But after I made my vows to live here forever, the abbess asked me to care for Sr. Celine. She has dementia and is with me all the time—24/7. At prayer time, Mass, and meals, she relies on me to show her what we're doing. I never get a break—I sleep in a bed next to her in case she wakes up and wanders off—and it can be a bit challenging. Even though I sometimes lose my patience and snap at her, she never ceases to shower me with love and affection.

"About a year ago, I was complaining to a priest about my dashed dreams of becoming a contemplative. He helped me to discover something I was totally unaware of. Sr. Celine has given me the experience of God's unconditional love that I had hoped to receive in prayer. She is a living reminder that I am always in the presence of unconditional love—and that was my original dream when I came to the monastery."

Sr. Carolyn's remark reminded me that God is a God of surprise and disguise. He knocks on the door of the heart in different ways—sometimes challenging—but always with the same intention: to give us an experience of unconditional love. We are called to open the heart's door and accept whatever God asks of us.

A Paradox

"I'm an emotional mess," José confided in me.

"What do you mean?"

"I've been intentional about my spiritual life for over a decade," he replied. "As I look back over the years, I can see how God's grace has touched me and even changed me. I can see how some virtues have taken root in my life.

"But the more I pray, the more I realize I'm an emotional mess. I see how my motivations are sometimes mixed and every now and then, I bump up against the dark side of my personality. You would think that after ten-plus years, my motivations would be pure and my dark side would have dissipated. But that has not happened. The more I invest in the spiritual life, the more I realize just how messed up I am."

I T'S A FACT IN THE SPIRITUAL LIFE THAT THE MORE WE COME TO KNOWLEDGE OF GOD, THE MORE WE COME TO SELF-KNOWLEDGE.

It's a fact in the spiritual life that the more we come to knowledge of God, the more we come to self-knowledge. And that self-knowledge includes how the weeds and wheat, to use the imagery from a parable of Jesus (see Matthew 13:24-30), have been planted in our hearts. As we grow spiritually, we become painfully aware of our mixed motivations, the dark side of our personalities, and how our childhood deficiency continues to hold a tight grip around our hearts.

Like many people's, José's understanding of holiness is a bit distorted and naïve. When I asked him to describe his understanding of sanctity, he replied, "It's when you have your act together and you are focused exclusively on God." It was as if he was suggesting that saints are incandescent people who glow in the dark and have resolved all their personality flaws and overcome all their idiosyncrasies, foibles, weaknesses, and quirks.

The reality is quite different: holy people and saints are not perfect. They are flawed. St. Jerome struggled with a fearful temper. St. Aloysius Gonzaga was known to be a party pooper and was quite severe, not knowing how to enjoy the things of this world. St. Thérèse of Lisieux was often tempted against charity. Mother Teresa of Calcutta struggled with control issues. These personality weaknesses and faults in no way take away from the fact that these people lived holy lives and are saints. A great paradox in the spiritual life is that saints-in-the-making and contemplatives in action are very much aware that they are flawed and sinful people who are desperately in need of a savior.

St. Paul bumped up against a character trait he wished he didn't have. Writing to the church in Corinth, he referred to it as "a thorn . . . in the flesh, a messenger of Satan to torment me" (2 Corinthians 12:7). This thorn and satanic messenger might have been a character flaw, a weakness, or an ongoing temptation. He wrote, "Three times I appealed to the Lord about this, that it would leave me, but he said to me, 'My grace is sufficient for you, for power is made perfect in weakness'" (12:8-9). Earlier in that same letter, he had written, "But we have this treasure in clay jars, so that it may be made clear that this extraordinary power belongs to God and does not come from us" (4:7).

Contemplatives in action are broken people who exude the power of God and God's grace. As they pray and grow in prayerfulness, grace gradually transforms them. That reality shines through as they grow in wonder and awe, live in the present moment, and grow in the attitudes of gratitude, generosity, and gentleness. Their hearts are stretched as they develop sensitivity for others, patience, and self-acceptance. And their lives are enriched by the experience of unconditional love when they set aside their personal agenda and respond to the daily divine invitations to help build the kingdom of peace, love, and justice.

REFLECTION QUESTIONS

1. How does my prayerfulness affect my relationships with family, friends, neighbors, and strangers?

2. Which characteristics of a contemplative in action mentioned in this chapter are present in my life? Which are missing?

3. In my opinion, what makes someone holy or a living saint?

10

WALKING WITH A SPIRITUAL DIRECTOR

An experienced spiritual director can be a wise asset for
the journey of prayer.

When I think back on my fifty-plus years of prayer, I am reminded of the spiritual directors who helped me navigate its challenges: Fr. Murray, Sr. Teresa, Fr. Robb, Mary Ann, Fr. Jude, Sr. Marguerite, Matthew, Br. Paul, and Lucille. At one point in my late twenties, I even considered Thomas Merton, the famed Trappist monk and spiritual writer of the twentieth century, as my spiritual director since I was reading just about every book he had written. Each person not only accompanied me on a particular segment of the journey but also offered unique insights. What always came as a surprise was that God placed the right spiritual director at my side at just the right moment. Having an experienced spiritual director kept me faithful to prayer as I struggled with distractions, dryness, and darkness. The spiritual directors also taught me how to open the door of my heart and respond to God's persistent invitations and requests.

A Misnomer

I sometimes think the label "spiritual director" is a misnomer. It unfortunately suggests someone like a conductor of a symphony who sets the tone of the directee's spiritual life, directing it and telling the person what to do and when. It suggests to some that the spiritual director will impose his or her prayer techniques or approach to the spiritual life on the directee. Some people even mistakenly believe that they must make a promise of obedience to their spiritual director.

Nothing could be further from the truth. There is only one spiritual director and that is the Holy Spirit. A man or woman who has been trained as a spiritual director, sometimes called a spiritual companion, *directs* your attention to the Holy Spirit and usually has more questions than answers. That's why the trained person is called a spiritual *director*. He or she attempts to heighten your attention and response to the God of surprise and disguise and the divine knock on the door of the heart.

That direction is made concrete in questions such as these:

- What is God saying to you in this feeling?
- How can you open the door of your heart even wider to God's grace?
- When did you last experience God like that?
- What do you think God might be inviting you to do in this situation?
- How are you praying with this experience?

Such open-ended questions are prompts that facilitate a person's prayerfulness and the awareness of the role one can play in the kingdom of peace, love, and justice.

These questions highlight the difference between a life coach, counselor, and spiritual director. A life coach helps a client to make better use of their time, talent, and potential. The life coach listens and offers techniques to improve the client's efficiency at home or in the office. A counselor also listens but helps the client negotiate painful emotions or unhealthy behaviors that block their psychological growth. Like a life coach and a counselor, a spiritual director also listens but with a very different intention: to help the directee grow in the awareness of God's invitations and to encourage a generous response for the sake of the kingdom.

Characteristics of a Spiritual Directee

When I first began as a spiritual director, I was convinced that spiritual direction was a practice that could be beneficial for anyone. But over the years, I've come to the minority opinion that not everyone is ripe for spiritual direction. Before committing to accompanying a person on the spiritual journey, I look for certain qualities in the person during the initial spiritual direction session. These qualities include the following:

- a commitment to daily prayer that isn't content with simply "saying prayers" but includes pondering and reflecting on how God might be using and speaking through people, events and situations, one's deepest feelings, and one's most creative thoughts;

- the willingness and ability to talk about prayer experiences, even when prayer is dry or the directee is shrouded in darkness;

- the ability to live with ambiguity and not seek cut-and-dried solutions to every question that arises on the spiritual journey;

- the freedom and courage to follow the lead of the God of surprise and disguise;

- no immediate need for psychological therapy or grief counseling.

Not every directee possesses all these characteristics, but I do look for the willingness to be open to them and to nurture them. Sometimes I suggest the person first seek out addiction counseling, short-term counseling, or grief counseling if I suspect a dangerous or traumatic, precipitating circumstance has led them to my door.

Characteristics of a Spiritual Director

"What should I be looking for in a spiritual director?" Amanda's question is worth noting. I suggest a few qualities are necessary:

- the ability to listen deeply and keep confidentiality;
- a wealth of life experience, including the transition through midlife;
- an appreciation for the myriad ways of God that makes the director hesitant to judge, condemn, or hold any personal bias or prejudice;
- an awareness of one's own strengths and weaknesses;
- the ability and willingness to let God take the lead in the directee's life;
- an understanding not only of the basic principles of discernment but also of the faith and spiritual traditions;
- has a spiritual director for himself or herself.

Like the characteristics of someone who is ripe for spiritual direction, these characteristics are not necessarily held by each trained spiritual director. But an experienced and wise spiritual director will certainly have a few of them.

"I guess my spiritual director should be a priest or religious sister, huh?" Amanda's second question implied a fallacy held by many.

I said to her, "No. There are many lay people—both Catholic and Protestant—who have been trained in the art of spiritual direction and who make wise spiritual companions. Many priests and religious sisters have not been trained. And many are just too busy to commit to being a spiritual companion. I suggest you contact three or four potential directors and have an initial interview. It's important that you feel a connection with your director. You'll get a sense of a possible connection as you ask them about their training, their approach to spiritual direction, and whether they have the time and interest to accompany you. Don't be offended if the person turns you down. It's just as important for your director to feel a connection with you as it is for you to have a connection with him or her."

Some Practicalities

I anticipated Amanda's third question. "How do I go about finding a spiritual director?"

"It's not as difficult as you might think," I said. "Put the word out to your relatives and friends. You'll be surprised when someone says, 'I hear so-and-so does spiritual direction or has a spiritual director.' Follow up on that lead. Check with your local church since many have trained spiritual directors on staff or have contact information of parishioners or church members who offer spiritual direction. If that doesn't produce any leads, check local convents, monasteries, retreat houses, or Christian conference centers. Many offer spiritual direction as an outreach to the community."

Another resource that many have discovered is the free website of Spiritual Directors International (www.sdicompanions.org). In the upper left-hand corner of the home page, click "Find" and scroll down to "Need Help Finding a Spiritual Director or Companion to Work With? Start Here." After reading some of the introductory questions and answers, click "Spiritual Director." You'll be asked to provide your spiritual orientation, the preferred gender of your potential director, language and age preferences, your city, and how far you are willing to travel. Once you have provided those parameters, the contact information for potential spiritual directors and companions who match your preferences will appear.

You might be surprised to discover that many spiritual directors and companions now offer virtual spiritual direction using online conference platforms such as Zoom, Skype, GoToMeeting, and Webex. That has become the preferred way of meeting for the vast majority of my own spiritual directees.

Amanda wasn't embarrassed to ask the fourth question that many hesitate to bring up. "How much does it cost?"

"There's two schools of thought on that, Amanda. Some people believe that spiritual direction is a ministry in the Church and, as such, shouldn't come with a cost. They like to quote the words of Jesus, 'You received without payment; give without payment' (Matthew 10:8).

"But other people have invested time and money into being trained as a spiritual director. They expect a stipend and might even have a fixed rate. For those like me who don't have a fixed rate, I suggest your hourly professional wage or what you consider the value of an hour of your time. And be aware that many spiritual directors would never turn you down for lack of funds."

The Spiritual Direction Session

"What exactly do you do in spiritual direction?" is a question that some people have asked me.

I always begin by stating the importance of the spiritual directee's preparation. If a directee has not prepared for the session, the spiritual director is forced to go on a fishing expedition to discover what's going on in the directee's life. That can be a waste of time and money.

How do you prepare for a session? Seven to ten days before the session, spend a few minutes each day asking, "What is God up to in my life? Where is the God of surprise and disguise knocking on the door of my heart? What is God asking of me?" As you ponder these three questions, the answers could lead you to reflect on a relationship that you're treasuring or struggling with, a situation you currently find yourself in, a deep-seated feeling that is recurring, or a creative thought that seemingly came out of nowhere. The answers to those questions will establish an agenda to bring to your spiritual director.

During your fifty-minute spiritual direction session, you'll begin by stating the *facts* of your agenda: for example, "I'm having some difficulties with my spouse."

Your director might ask your *feelings* and emotional response to this agenda item. You might reply, "I'm frustrated and don't always understand what's going on between us." Sometimes the feelings might have to be explored for a few minutes.

After you have mentioned your emotional response, the director will lead you to the arena of *faith* where the session is typically centered: for example, your director might ask, "What do you think God is saying to you in your frustration? What is God now asking of you in the relationship with your spouse? How are you praying with this period of frustration?" As you and your director explore the faith dimension of your agenda item, various appropriate actions and responses will naturally come up. You'll then be able to strategize, discern, and decide the best course of action for the sake of God's kingdom.

Not all spiritual direction sessions are this neat and tidy, however. Occasionally more time is needed to understand the facts and process the subsequent feelings that arose. But ideally, the intent is to move from the facts through the feelings to the faith level because this third level facilitates a prayerful attitude to all dimensions of one's life.

DON'T BE SURPRISED IF AFTER TWO, THREE, OR FOUR YEARS, YOU OUTGROW YOUR SPIRITUAL DIRECTOR. THAT'S NATURAL.

Three Basic Goals

There are three important goals of spiritual direction.

First, by accompanying the directee on the journey of prayer, the spiritual director can help broaden the directee's understanding of the spiritual life. Sooner or later, fidelity to prayer leads to the discovery that all of life is spiritual. This is prayerfulness, the ultimate purpose of prayer.

The second goal is to encourage the directee to open the door of the heart ever wider to the God of surprise and disguise. In practical terms, this leads to the prayer of Jesus, "Your will be done" (see Luke 22:42). The directee discerns and discovers a personal mission given by God to help foster the kingdom of peace, love, and justice. The spiritual director encourages the person to overcome the fear of "getting it wrong" and grow in the willingness to take a faith-filled risk.

Third, spiritual darkness causes pain and confusion as the directee is challenged to detach from the idols of the heart and has his or her image of God purified. The spiritual director walks as a witness to the reality that spiritual darkness is the *other* side of grace.

One final note on spiritual direction is worth noting. Don't be surprised if after two, three, or four years, you outgrow your spiritual director. That's natural. When you find yourself knowing what your director will say or you find your sessions unproductive, it might be time to move on to a new spiritual director or companion. Experienced spiritual directors expect this and are eager for you to continue the journey with someone else. So don't fear you will be hurting their feelings.

It's a wonderful gift to your spiritual director if, in the final session, you trace the history of your spiritual journey and what you have learned from the director's wisdom and experience.

Spiritual direction plays a vital role in the lives of many who are intent on listening for God's persistent knocking on the heart's door and discovering their unique role in building the kingdom. It's a concrete witness that we never walk the spiritual journey alone. It also provides encouragement on the faith walk, especially in times of testing, trials, and darkness.

Reflection Questions

1. What has been my experience with spiritual direction? Was it a help or hindrance to my life of prayer? Why?

2. What aspects of my life would I feel hesitant or uncomfortable discussing with a spiritual director? Why?

3. What qualities and characteristics do I think are most important for a spiritual director who accompanies me on the spiritual journey? Why those?

Conclusion

I once asked Ryan and Yvonne, happily married for fifty-two years, the secret to a successful marriage.

"The three Cs," Ryan replied.

"The three Cs?" I asked, looking at Yvonne.

"Commitment, communication, . . ." she said.

". . . and compromise," Ryan finished her reply.

Like any other intimate relationship, our relationship with God requires commitment, communication, and compromise.

We commit to spending time with God in daily prayer. That is how a relationship begins and matures. During our time with God, we discover what prayer methods are suitable and personally satisfying—as well as how much time we should spend in a typical prayer period. This takes some trial and error.

During our prayer time, we communicate with God. We get out of our heads and pray from the neck down. That requires opening the door of our heart and sharing with God the details of our day and the feelings and emotions that arise. With the windows of the soul open, we also petition and intercede for others. Nothing is off-limits when it comes to our conversation with God. Over time, our words become inadequate as we open our heart's door even wider to the silence of lovers.

Like any other relationship, our relationship with God requires compromise. We let go of any expectations or personal agenda we might have. We are content to pray from where we are and not from where we think we should be. This includes the willingness to sit in spiritual darkness if invited. We become aware that spiritual darkness is a grace that detaches the heart from its idols and purifies it of any residual pride. Spiritual darkness also transforms our tightly held images of God.

Ultimately, our commitment to prayer with its accompanying communication and willingness to compromise should make us prayerful—that is, aware and attentive to the visits of a God of surprise and disguise. Like the persistent widow found in Jesus' parable (see Luke 18:1-5), God comes into our daily lives and knocks on the heart's door with the hope that we will open it and respond to the invitation to build the kingdom of peace, love, and justice.

Nine Principles of Prayer

1. Prayer should make me prayerful.

2. I need to find my own way to pray.

3. I pray from where I am and not from where I think I should be.

4. I petition God and intercede for others as expressions of my care, concern, and compassion. I do not try to convince or coax a change in God's will.

5. Frustration and burnout in prayer are signs that I am trying too hard.

6. Growth in prayer is moving from words to silence.

7. Spiritual darkness is a grace that facilitates detachment and purification.

8. Fidelity to prayer, while reminding me of my brokenness, transforms my lifestyle from compulsion to contemplation.

9. An experienced spiritual director can be a wise asset for the journey of prayer.

A List of Prayer Techniques Discussed

Chapter 1

- Pastor Joe's Ten-Minute Prayer
- The Examen
- The Daily Check-In

Chapter 2

- Scriptural Quotations
- The Jesus Prayer
- The Hail Mary
- *Lectio Divina*
- The Four Hs Prayer
- Imaginative Prayer
- ACTS
- *Visio Divina*

Chapter 3

- The Prayer of the Heart
- The Welcoming Prayer
- Come as You Are Prayer
- The Psalms
- The Stations of the Cross

Chapter 4

- Praying the News
- The World Mission Rosary
- Forgiving God

Chapter 5

- The Prayer of Just Sitting

Chapter 6

- Praying with Creation
- The Jesus Prayer
- Centering Prayer
- Christian Meditation
- Mystical Prayer

Chapter 7

- The Prayer of Job

Chapter 8

- St. Charles de Foucauld's Prayer of Abandonment

Notes

[1]   William McNamara as quoted by Walter J. Burghardt, "Contemplation: A Long, Loving Look at the Real," *Church,* No. 5 (Winter 1989): 14-17.

[2]   St. John Damascene, *De fide orth.* 3, 24; PG 94, 1089C.

[3]   St. Augustine, Sermon 52, 6, 16: PL 38, 360, and Sermon 117, 3, 5: PL 38, 663.

[4]   The expression was coined by Jerome Nadal, an early follower of St. Ignatius of Loyola.

About the Author

Ordained a Franciscan priest in 1983, Albert Haase, OFM, is a popular preacher and teacher. A former missionary to mainland China for over eleven years, he is the award-winning author of more than fifteen books on popular spirituality and the presenter on five bestselling streaming videos (Paraclete Press). He currently resides in San Antonio, TX. Visit his website at www.AlbertOFM.org

Other Books and Media by Albert Haase, OFM

- *Swimming in the Sun: Rediscovering the Lord's Prayer with Francis of Assisi and Thomas Merton* (St. Anthony Messenger Press, 1993)

- *Enkindled: Holy Spirit, Holy Gifts,* coauthored with Bridget Haase, OSU (St. Anthony Messenger Press, 2001)

- *Instruments of Christ: Reflections on the Peace Prayer of St. Francis of Assisi* (St. Anthony Messenger Press, 2004)

- *Coming Home to Your True Self: Leaving the Emptiness of False Attractions* (InterVarsity Press, 2008)

- *Living the Lord's Prayer: The Way of the Disciple* (InterVarsity Press, 2009)

- *The Lord's Prayer: A Summary of the Entire Gospel* (streaming audio) (Learn25.com, 2010)

- *This Sacred Moment: Becoming Holy Right Where You Are* (InterVarsity Press, 2011)

- *The Life of Antony of Egypt: By Athanasius, A Paraphrase* (InterVarsity Press, 2012)

- *Catching Fire, Becoming Flame: A Guide for Spiritual Transformation* (Paraclete Press, 2013)

- *Catching Fire, Becoming Flame: A Guide for Spiritual Transformation* (streaming video) (Paraclete Press, 2013)

- *Keeping the Fire Alive: Navigating Challenges in the Spiritual Life* (streaming video) (Paraclete Press, 2014)

- *Come, Follow Me: Six Responses to the Call of Jesus* (streaming video) (Paraclete Press, 2014)

- *Saying Yes: Discovering and Responding to God's Will in Your Life* (Paraclete Press, 2016)

- *Saying Yes: What Is God's Will for Me?* (streaming video) (Paraclete Press, 2016)

- *Practical Holiness: Pope Francis as Spiritual Companion* (Paraclete Press, 2019)

- *Becoming an Ordinary Mystic: Spirituality for the Rest of Us* (InterVarsity Press, 2019)

- *Soul Training with the Peace Prayer of Saint Francis* (Franciscan Media, 2020)

- *Sundays on the Go: 90 Seconds with the Weekly Gospel, Year A* (Paraclete Press, 2022)

- *Catching Fire, Becoming Flame: A Guide for Spiritual Transformation. Tenth Anniversary Edition. Revised and Expanded* (Paraclete Press, 2022)

- *Touching the Bones of Elisha: Nine Life-Giving Spiritual Practices from an Ancient Prophet*, coauthored with Phil Vestal (Cascade Books, 2023)

- *Sundays on the Go: 90 Seconds with the Weekly Gospel, Year B* (Paraclete Press, 2023)

- *Sundays on the Go: 90 Seconds with the Weekly Gospel, Year C* (Paraclete Press, 2024)

theWORD
among us®

The Word Among Us publishes a monthly devotional magazine, books, Bible studies, and pamphlets that help Catholics grow in their faith.

To learn more about who we are and what we publish, visit www.wau.org. There you will find a variety of Catholic resources that will help you grow in your faith.

Your review makes a difference! If you enjoyed this book, please consider sharing your review on Amazon using the QR code below.

*Embrace His Word
Listen to God . . .*

www.wau.org

Made in the USA
Las Vegas, NV
12 February 2024

85663200R00085